HOW TO FORM YOUR OWN ILLINOIS CORPORATION *BEFORE THE INC. DRIES!*

A Step-by-Step Guide, With Forms

by *Phillip G. Williams, Ph.D.*

How to Incorporate a Small Business Series
Volume 1

sixth, updated edition

The P. Gaines Co.
PO Box 2253, Oak Park, Illinois 60303
Telephone (708) 524-9033

Library of Congress Cataloging-in-Publication Data

Williams, Phil, 1946-
    How to form your own Illinois corporation before the inc. dries! : a step-by-step guide, with forms / by Phillip G. Williams. — 6th updated ed.
        p.   cm. – (How to incorporate a small business series : v.1)
    Includes index.
    ISBN 0-936284-27-7 (paperback)
     1.Incorporation—Illinois—Popular works. 2. Corporation law—Illinois—Popular works.
    I.Title. II. Series.

    KF11413.5.Z9W54 2003
    346.773'06622--dc21

                           2002191904

Cover design by Anne O'Connor, Oak Park, Illinois

Manufactured in the United States of America

Table of Contents

Introduction

If you are thinking of starting your own small business or have already done so, you may find yourself perplexed by the large number of laws governing your business activities. At one time, doing business in the United States was a much simpler affair. Most business activity consisted of small manufacturers and merchants offering their wares and services on a local or regional basis.

Today, the trend is toward economic concentration in the hands of a small number of multinational corporations, who own everything from breakfast cereal firms to computer manufacturers.

We are also experiencing, on the other hand, a rediscovery of the individual entrepreneur, who has become a new kind of folk hero. Even large corporations at present are trying to tap into the strengths of entrepreneurial thinking. Some have designated individuals or even whole departments to work independently from the rest of the company in quest of more creative approaches to their business problems.

While some of the most astute large corporations are promoting entrepreneurial values as part of their own structure, many entrepreneurs find themselves in need of following the opposite path. They stand to gain from learning the techniques of business that major corporations practice.

Incorporation itself is one such practice that many small businesses are learning to profitably adapt to their own purposes.

We may wistfully recall the past and may even work for a reduction in our increasingly unwieldy business and tax regulations, but we cannot completely turn back the clock. With greater complexity and sophistication of techniques here to stay, many small businesses wish to take advantage of the corporate form of operation.

A number of individuals as well as businesses can benefit from organizing their own corporation. Persons in administrative and consulting positions can often profitably quit their present jobs, form their own corporate firms, and sell their services back to their employers, to the advantage of both parties. Salespeople, writers, artists, and designers will, in many cases, stand to gain from incorporating, as will many others planning to start or already running their own businesses, whether it be a catering service or a construction firm. Professionals such as engineers, dentists, and architects may profit from incorporating their practices as well.

Some of the advantages of incorporation include:

- limited liability
- greater financial flexibility
- a low corporate income tax rate for retained earnings

- a host of tax-free benefits, such as: tax-free life insurance, a medical and dental plan paying all expenses, including drug costs and health insurance, a tax-deductible salary-continuation and disability plan, a tuition reimbursement plan, free legal services, and corporate stock dividends that are 70 percent tax free.

The present book, designed to clarify the important business area of incorporation, is written specifically for Illinois individuals and businesses, providing a thorough discussion of the advantages and disadvantages of incorporation, tax angles, employee benefits, and a blueprint for setting up your own Illinois corporation.

In the back of this book, we provide in appendices all the forms necessary to organize an Illinois corporation. For ease of use, with this new edition of the book we are also supplying all the incorporation forms on our web site at www.PGaines.com .

Chapter 5 covers the procedure for forming a profit corporation, while Chapter 7 deals with the not-for-profit corporation. If you wish to form an Illinois professional service corporation as a doctor, veterinarian, dentist, public accountant, psychologist, engineer, architect, or other licensed professional, you will find this type of corporation explained in Chapter 6.

If you prefer to do your own incorporation without a lawyer, you are entitled to do so, since you are not required by Illinois law to use an attorney to incorporate your business. Since the average attorney fee for an incorporation runs from $400 to $2,500, you will save money by incorporating yourself.

On the other hand, if you already have a prospering business and little time to concern yourself with the details of incorporating, you can find a competent attorney in your area through the local chapter of the American Bar Association.

If you do prefer to use the services of a lawyer to handle your incorporation, the information provided herein will help you ask the right questions of your attorney and make the most informed decisions. If you decide to fill out and file your own incorporation papers, we recommend having a lawyer review them, since even simple incorporations may have complications. You will still save money by following this review procedure, since the charge for this service at an hourly rate (approximately $100 to $150) will be substantially less than the full incorporation fee.

If there are aspects to your incorporation not treated in the following discussion, we also advise legal consultation prior to filing the Articles of Incorporation.

Chapter 1. Four Forms of Business Ownership

Until recently, the federal and state governments of the United States and their agents such as the IRS have recognized three legal forms of business ownership: the sole proprietorship, the partnership, and the corporation. All fifty states have recently adopted yet a fourth form of business operation, called the limited liability company.[1] While this book is primarily concerned with the category of the corporation, it is important to examine the other three by way of comparison. Each has distinct advantages and disadvantages.

Sole Proprietorship

If you operate your own business and have not incorporated, organized as an LLC, or entered into a partnership agreement, you are automatically classified as a sole proprietor. In other words, a sole proprietor is one person engaged in a business for profit. The chief advantage of this form of operation is its informality. You can start or terminate your business whenever you feel like it. The state or federal government cannot prevent you from starting this type of business, so long as it is not illegal.

The sole proprietor can also freely mix personal and business finances, lumping all the money into one bank account or handling it however he or she pleases. Of course, the sole proprietor, like all business owners, has to pay taxes so she must apply for a state sales tax number, keep records, file state and federal tax returns and follow all other procedures required by law. But as the least regulated of the four forms of business ownership, the sole proprietorship does not require permission from the state for its formation, operation, or dissolution.

Furthermore, the sole proprietor may transfer the inventory of his business to personal use. In the case of the corner grocery store, the owner may simply choose to eat what he does not sell. If the store owner wants to take a chicken from his meat case or a cantaloupe from his fruit stand, he is free to do so.[2]

---

[1] While offering the advantage of limited liability, like a corporation, the limited liability company is structured like a partnership and sometimes requires a minimum of two persons to form. Illinois is one of the states to authorize this type of business entity. The highlights of the provisions of that law are discussed in the section below on the "Limited Liability Company."

---

[2] It should be noted, however, that even the sole proprietor is required, for tax purposes, to keep a record of inventory adopted for personal use.

The major disadvantage of the sole proprietorship is that the owner is personally liable for all the debts of the business and for any injuries caused to or by its employees acting in a business capacity. If your warehouse clerk drops a 50-gallon drum on the head of one of your customers, for example, then you are personally responsible for the damages.[3]

Therefore, as sole proprietor, not just your business assets are "at risk." If you owe creditors more than your business is worth or if a legal suit against you awards the plaintiff an amount in excess of your business assets, your personal assets as well—your bank account, your car, your home, your Persian rugs— may all be legally attached, and your salary garnisheed if you have other employment as well.[4] Your liability as a sole proprietor is limited only by the totality of all your possessions, personal as well as business.

Realistically speaking, many small businesses have no choice but to start existence as a sole proprietorship, if the owner does not have sufficient time and resources to deal with the greater complexity entailed by the corporate form of operation. If the enterprise prospers, however, incorporation will become, in time, an increasingly attractive option.

Expert Advice on Sole Proprietorships and Accounting

An excellent book on starting and running a sole proprietorship is **Small Time Operator: How to Start Your Own Business, Keep Your Books, Pay Your Taxes, and Stay Out of Trouble!** *by Bernard Kamoroff, C.P.A. This book also includes a thorough treatment of accounting practices for the small business (whether incorporated or unincorporated) and contains enough actual ledger sheets and worksheets to last a full year. This publication can be ordered from The P. Gaines Co. See the order form in the back of this book.*

This information is needed in completing the 1040 Schedule C form.

[3] Insurance is one means of protection, although it is often an expensive way to limit personal liability. It may also be virtually impossible for the small business person to obtain at affordable rates. While corporations as well as sole proprietors generally carry insurance, if they can get it, the corporate form itself is a valuable protection against unlimited liability (with the exception of professional service corporations— See Chapter 6).

[4] Every state has laws that exempt certain personal possessions from attachment to satisfy debts, so a creditor cannot literally take the clothes off your back. Chapter 7 debtors faced with liquidation of their assets have exemptions of $5,000 on their home ($10,000 for married couples), $1,000 on their car, and, under federal law, $1,500 on any implements, professional books, or trade tools.

Partnership

A partnership is a business for profit owned by two or more individuals. Partnerships resemble sole proprietorships, with special allowances demanded by the fact of more than one owner. Thus, the same advantages enjoyed by the sole proprietor apply to the partnership as well, the lack of formal requirements being the chief benefit. There exist no special procedures for establishing a partnership; a simple verbal agreement is sufficient, although a written agreement in the event of future disagreements is highly advisable.

Termination of the partnership is automatic upon the death, disability, or withdrawal of one of the partners (unless otherwise agreed). Another important advantage of the partnership is that it provides a framework for individuals to pool their resources, including money, skills, and ideas. "We'll pool our resources and buy two horses--and a mule," as my old partner used to sing. In a partnership, the sum is often greater than the parts, since it permits persons acting together to achieve goals that none could attain individually.

The federal government's Uniform Partnership Act defines a partnership as "an association of two or more persons as co-owners of a business for profit." This act regulates the activities of partnerships in every state. It stipulates that the partners share equally in the profits and the losses, unless otherwise agreed. In a partnership, each partner owes the partnership a fiduciary duty to put the business interests of the partnership first. If partnership business is being siphoned off by one of the partners for his own use without the knowledge and consent of the other partners, that particular partner is guilty of defrauding the partnership and may be sued by the other principals.

As in the case of the sole proprietor, the partnership must follow all procedures, keep all records, and remit all forms and payments required by the state and federal taxing authorities. The partnership itself is not a taxable entity, however. The partnership annually reports its income to the IRS on an informational return (Form 1065), and the individual partners include their share of the profits on their personal 1040 tax returns. Thus a partnership determines its income and pays taxes basically the same way as an individual sole proprietor.

Like the sole proprietor also, the chief disadvantage of the partnership is the personal liability of each partner for the debts of the partnership. All partners in a business are individually liable for all acts of the business. If your partner(s) is (are) unscrupulous or unwise, you stand to lose a great deal more than your initial investment.

In summary, the risks of partnerships are extensive, since partners have unlimited liability for all actions or omissions of the partnership or its individual partners, employees, or others acting in its name and behalf.

Another disadvantage: When the assets of the partners are disproportionate and you are the partner with much greater assets, you stand to forfeit more in the event the partnership assets are inadequate to satisfy creditors' claims. In such an eventuality, your house may be attached and liquidated to pay business debts, whereas your undercapitalized partner may lose only her truck! Another disadvantage of the partnership is that each individual partner's profits are taxed in the year of receipt, whereas the corporate structure offers greater financial flexibility, often allowing you to spread profits over a number of years and thus reduce the tax bite.

Finally, under the Uniform Partnership Act there exists a special type of partnership called the "limited partnership," which combines aspects of a partnership and a corporation. A limited partnership has two classes of partners, defined as general and limited partners. The general partners assume the operation of the business. In a regular partnership, discussed above, all the partners are general partners. A limited partner, on the other hand, can invest in a partnership without involvement in its management and without the risk of personal liability. Unlike the general partner who has unlimited personal liability, the liability of the limited partner does not exceed the amount of his initial investment. Unlike a regular partnership, a limited partnership agreement, according to state law, can only be established in writing. Many types of real estate investment groups and oil and gas exploration projects, for instance, will have both general partners who organize the venture and limited

partners who invest in it. Interestingly, a marriage is considered a general partnership unless there is written agreement in advance that it is to be treated as a limited partnership!

Let's Shake on It!

The Partnership Book *by Denis Clifford and Ralph Warner provides an excellent source of information about the nuts and bolts of setting up effective partnership agreements. It covers evaluation of partnership assets, disputes, buy-outs, and the death of a partner. This publication can be ordered from The P. Gaines Co. Please see the order form in the back of this book for details.*

Important Note

In general, corporations often work much better than partnerships for many types of businesses. One type of business for which a partnership or limited liability company format may prove more advantageous is that of the professional firm. If you are a doctor or a lawyer or other kind of professional practitioner, you should explore with a skilled legal adviser whether a partnership or limited liability company structure offers particular advantages for you. In the areas of retirement payments and firm breakups, for instance, partnerships and LLCs may benefit the professional firm in ways not available to the corporation. See Chapter 6, "The Illinois Professional Service Corporation," for more discussion on this point.

12

Limited Liability Company

Contrary to the proverb, there *is* something new under the sun, the limited liability company. In 1991, only eight states recognized this form of busines operation. Today, all fifty states, including Illinois, authorize the formation of LLCs. Combining features of a corporation and a partnership, the LLC allows its owners to enjoy the limited liability of the corporate structure while being taxed like a partnership. Thus, the income or loss of the LLC flows through to the individual owners, usually in proportion to their holdings, and appears on their personal income tax returns. The LLC in Illinois no longer requires a minimum of two organizers, like a partnership. A single individual can now form an LLC in Illinois, effective January 1, 2001.

What would be the advantage of forming an LLC instead of a corporation? In many situations, there would be no tax advantage, since an S corporation would give you the same tax structure as an LLC: the income or loss from the S corporation is divvied up among the individual owners just like a partnership or an LLC.

From an organizational standpoint, however, LLCs are much easier to form and administer than S corporations. A host of complex rules govern the establishment and maintenance of S corporations. Breaking one of these rules may result in the dissolution of the S corporation, with unfavorable tax consequences. In the case of LLCs, however, what you see is what you get. Once the LLC is formed, you don't have to petition the IRS for special tax status in order to be taxed like a partnership, as in the case of S corporations. You will automatically be taxed as a partnership. You cannot accidentally lose your partnership tax status, furthermore, by violating an obscure rule, as in the case of an S corporation.

As pointed out in the section on Partnerships above, professional firms, especially ones with numerous owners, might find the limited liability company structure more suited to their particular needs. The S corporation is limited to 75 shareholders; LLCs have no limitations on the number of members they may have. In addition, LLCs offer certain advantages to professional firms in the areas of retirement payouts and firm breakups that the S corporation cannot match. See Chapter 6, "The Illinois Professional Service Corporation."

Another situation in which the formation of an LLC proves ideal is one involving joint ventures. Say, for instance, that a graphic designer and a printing company want to form a joint venture to sell a line of greeting cards. A partnership is one option, but an LLC has the obvious advantage of limited liability. If the greeting card venture folded and creditors were owed substantial amounts, in the case of a general partnership, the creditors could go after the assets of the individual partners. With an LLC, however, this is not the case. The personal assets of each of the members would be off limits to creditors seeking to recover debts incurred by the LLC.

The original Act authorizing LLCs in Illinois went into effect in 1994. The LLC is particularly well suited for foreign investment, venture capital, joint ventures, real estate, oil and gas and high technology transactions. If you plan to be involved in any ventures of this type, we recommend that you explore the advantages and disadvantages of this type of operation, compared to the corporate form of doing business, with a competent legal adviser.

Given Illinois's allowance of the right of single individuals to form LLCs, LLCs also offer an attractive choice to sole proprietors in the state, allowing them to limit personal liability without involving the greater complexity of the corporate form of business organization. There is one major drawback to setting up an LLC in Illinois, the cost. Most states have exactly the same fee structure to set up an LLC or a corporation. But in Illinois the fee to form an LLC is $400, down from $500, but still substantially more than the $100 fee required to set up a corporation.

Corporation

A corporation is a legal entity separate from its owner(s), manager(s), or operator(s). As a "legal person," it can conduct business, borrow and lend money, sue and be sued. Wanda Gold decides to incorporate her business and forms Wanda Gold Enterprises, Inc. Although Wanda is the sole owner and operator, her corporation in the eyes of the state has a distinct life of its own, separate from that of Wanda. It will be expected to pay taxes like a real person, it may enter into contracts, be named as a defendant or plaintiff in a lawsuit, acquire and hold property, and so on.

Unlike the sole proprietorship and the partnership, a corporation cannot be formed until you receive written approval from the state. The life of a corporation, its "birth," begins with the issuance of the Articles of Incorporation by the Secretary of State and ends with its voluntary or involuntary dissolution (as in the case of bankruptcy). The Illinois corporation statutes define the rules and procedures governing the formation, continuance, and termination of Illinois corporations.

Before we examine the mechanics of setting up your own corporation, however, let's take a closer look at the corporation as a form of business ownership.

Limited Liability
The majority of individuals forming Illinois corporations will enjoy the advantage of limiting personal liability by means of the corporate structure. Limiting liability, in fact, is traditionally one of the greatest incentives for incorporating a business. A corporate owner or director is not, in most cases, personally liable for the debts of the corporation. Therefore, if a lawsuit is brought against Wanda Gold Enterprises, Inc., only the assets of the corporation itself will be subject to collection, not the personal assets of Wanda herself (with certain important exceptions noted hereafter). This fact

14

can be very comforting to someone just starting out in business.

From the standpoint of limiting liability, the corporate route may be worth it in terms of peace of mind alone. Not only will the owner and other stockholders not be liable for the debts of the corporation, over and above their investment in the corporation in the form of shares of stock. Risk ventures can also be undertaken with the same assurances—only the investment of the corporation will be "at risk," not personal property.

In the event of a financial disaster, corporations, like individuals, can go bankrupt. If your corporation suddenly owes creditors half a million dollars and the assets of the company are only $20 thousand, then the business could file for bankruptcy. Once the $20 thousand in assets was distributed to creditors, the bankruptcy court would declare the corporation to be legally dissolved and the remainder of the company debt would, in effect, be wiped out. You would then be free to start another corporation tomorrow with a new name, if you so desired.

This is not, of course, a recommendation that you form a corporation and amass huge debts and then cancel them out by filing for bankruptcy. Not only would such an intentional attempt to evade payment of bills be unethical. But most creditors would be unwilling to extend a large line of credit to you in the first place unless you were an established customer.

If it were apparent, moreover, that you intentionally formed a "thin" (undercapitalized) corporation in order to avoid payment of debts, you would in all probability not escape personal liability. The courts in such cases in the past have tended to subject the shareholders of such corporations to personal liability. The point is that, in the event of a major unforeseeable disaster—a lawsuit, large casualty loss, and so on—bankruptcy is a final "escape clause" for corporations which, unlike the sole proprietorship and the partnership, allows your personal assets to remain untouched.

The cases in which liability is *not* limited by the corporate structure generally fall into one of three categories:
  (1) taxes
  (2) instances of gross negligence, fraud, mismanagement, or malpractice (especially in the case of professional service corporations)
  (3) personal assets pledged to secure a loan

Regarding the matter of taxes, remember that the payment of taxes is the lifeblood of the state and federal governments. Strict laws and penalties safeguard this form of governmental livelihood. In this delicate area, even corporations are not exempt from sanctions, and, in some situations, an officer or employee of a corporation can be held personally liable for failure to withhold and pay taxes.[5]

---

[5] If this is one of the defined duties of the employee's position, as treasurer, for instance.

Second, professional malfeasance may also trigger personal liability, as in the case of a director or officer who mismanages or takes advantage of the corporation.[6] This type of misconduct most often involves plundering the corporate assets through actual theft or other instances of draining the company's financial reserves. Not giving the corporation the "right of first refusal" also falls under this category.

Other fraudulent acts, such as "doctoring" the corporate balance sheets, may result in personal liability as well. In such situations, the corporation can sue the individual in question, who will be subject to personal financial liability for losses that he caused to the corporation. In addition to actual damages, the courts may also assess punitive damages, and the guilty party may also be subject to criminal prosecution. Several large American corporations, such as Enron and Worldcom, have seen their stock prices nosedive after the discovery of such irregularities with their earnings accounts.

Under the same heading, it is important to realize that professional service corporations do not enjoy the same advantage as other types of corporations.[7] A doctor or lawyer who has incorporated his practice, for example, will still be personally liable for any acts of professional misconduct,

including malpractice, in his or her role as a practitioner of the profession. (The Illinois professional association law does not remove the limited liability of the professional as a shareholder of the corporation, however.) This does not mean that incorporating does not offer other advantages to professionals. It sometimes does, so that individual professionals may find incorporating an advantage. See Chapter 6 for a detailed discussion of the Illinois Professional Service Corporation.

Third, creditors such as banks naturally want to limit their risks as much as possible. An owner of a small corporation will often be asked to pledge personal assets as security for a loan. Obviously, the shield for personal assets which the corporate form provides in other situations will not work in this case.

In spite of these three exceptions, the corporation does offer a limitation of liability not available to the sole proprietor or partnership. In the event of legal damages you must pay, owing to injury or loss to consumers caused by goods or services you manufacture or sell, your corporation will serve as a reliable umbrella, in most cases protecting your personal assets from attachment and liquidation. This advantage alone may be worth the price of incorporation for most individuals.

---

[6] We are not speaking here of honest errors in judgment but of gross negligence and downright intent to defraud.

[7] Professions authorized by the Illinois Professional Service Corporation Act include all licensed professions, such as architecture, engineering, and medicine in all its branches.

The Corporation as a Tax Shelter
The corporation as a form of business ownership can save taxes in a number of ways not available to the sole proprietor or partnership, including corporate income tax rates lower than personal ones, corporate pension[8] and profit-sharing plans, corporate medical reimbursement plans, and other allowable business deductions.

The following examples show how federal income tax savings may be realized and income generated by incorporating, through a combination of lower corporate tax rates, benefit plans, and the structuring of the sale of a going business to the new corporation. The current graduated federal tax rate for corporations taxes the first $50,000 of income at 15 percent, income of $50,000 to $75,000 at a 25 percent rate, and income over $75,000 at a 34 percent[9] rate. (An additional 5 percent tax, up to $11,750, is imposed on corporate taxable income over $100,000. Corporations with taxable income of at least $335,000 pay a flat rate of 34 percent.) A corporation would pay $7,500 in federal taxes on $50,000 in income, for example, while a single individual would pay $9,853 at present in federal taxes on the same dollar amount.

Example 1
If Wanda Gold (a single individual) has $40,000 in taxable income, she would pay $7,153 in federal income tax, whereas Wanda Gold Enterprises, Inc. with the same taxable income would pay only $6,000 in federal taxes. Tax savings are only the tip of the iceberg, furthermore.

Consider the following situation. If Wanda Gold Enterprises, Inc. pays Wanda a salary of $25,000 for her services to the corporation, she would personally owe $3,454 in federal income tax under current rates. If her corporation showed a profit of $40,000 for the year, Wanda's salary, assuming it is "reasonable," would be deductible from the amount as a necessary business expense, thus reducing to $15,000 the income taxable to the corporation.

If the corporation has a retirement plan, a profit-sharing plan, and a medical reimbursement plan,[10] however, the contributions of the corporation to each of these plans would also reduce dollar-for-dollar the corporation's taxable income. Each of these plans would provide a form of tax-free income to

---

[8] The 1982 tax act in effect eliminated much of the past favoritism of corporate retirement plans over Keogh plans for the self-employed sole proprietor, but the tax shelter advantages of all such plans remain immense. In one area, discussed in Chapter 4, the defined benefit corporation retirement plan still offers advantages over other plans for nonincorporated businesses.

[9] The Clinton tax act of 1993 did create another, higher tax bracket for corporations (35 percent bracket), but this rate applies only to corporations with taxable income over $10 million.

[10] An individual taxpayer can also deduct medical, dental, and prescription drug expenses, as well as medical insurance premiums, if he itemizes deductions, but only to the extent that such expenses, when lumped together, exceed 7.5 percent of adjusted gross income. As a result, many individual taxpayers receive no deduction for medical expenses.

Wanda (while some of it would be direct income, some would be deferred income).

At the same time, the corporation could deduct the full amount of its contributions as ordinary expenses. If Wanda Gold Enterprises, Inc. pays out $9,000 during the year in medical reimbursements and pension and profit-sharing plan contributions for Wanda, for instance, it will show only $6,000 in taxable income (it will owe only $900 in corporate federal tax, in other words). Taking into consideration Wanda's individual income tax of $3,454 paid on her salary and the corporate tax of $900, a total tax of $4,354 will be paid for the year.

Don't forget that Wanda would have to pay $7,153 in taxes if she were on a straight salary of $40,000. She would enjoy a federal tax savings of $2,799 in this particular instance because of the corporate structure. Remember also that Wanda will gain $9,000 from the corporation in non-taxable benefits for that particular year as well, over and above the straight tax savings. Wanda's company could contribute up to $600 to her favorite charity, moreover, and deduct it from income as a business expense.

Example 2
You decide to incorporate a going business whose worth has been appraised at $220,000. By carefully structuring the sale of your sole proprietorship to your corporation, you can provide yourself a substantial,

almost totally tax-free income for a number of years.

Here's how one such plan might work. Accept only a small portion of the total value of the business, say, $40,000, in stock from the newly formed corporation. For the remaining $180,000, take back a note from the corporation. (You are lending the corporation the additional $180,000 to buy the business, in other words.) If the term of the note is set for four years, you will receive principal and interest from the note over the next four years, with only the interest portion taxable (the rest the IRS considers a nontaxable return of principal). The major portion of the proceeds ($45,000 from return of principal each year) will escape taxes.

The above examples illustrate some of the many tax-saving devices available to corporations. These strategies will be discussed further in Chapter 4, "Taxes and the Corporation as a Tax Shelter."

Perpetual Existence, Formality, and the Corporate Image
Unlike a sole proprietorship or partnership that ends with the death, disability, or withdrawal of the owner(s), a corporation may have a virtually unending life of its own. This aspect of the corporation we refer to as its "perpetual existence."

Of course, you can voluntarily terminate a corporation if you, the owner, choose to dissolve it because of financial or personal reasons. Also, a bankruptcy proceeding, as mentioned, may result in involuntary dissolution. These exceptions notwithstanding, the corporation is a more stable form of business than the sole proprietorship or partnership because its life is independent of a particular owner or management team.

Besides increased stability, the corporate form also requires greater formality of business operation. This is the positive side to the larger number of regulations governing corporations, as compared to other types of businesses. Symbolic of this increased formality is the use of the corporate seal on business agreements, such as the application for a corporate bank account or a corporate loan application.[11]

The stability and formality of the corporate form will help to lend credence and authority to your business in the eyes of creditors, banks, employees, and customers. Just as good will is an intangible yet very important asset to your business, so too does the corporate image play a valuable role.

If you are involved, for example, in consulting, free-lance writing, editing, advertising, or other types of loosely structured businesses, the Inc. after your company name may very well give you a decided edge over your competitors. The fact that you have chosen to incorporate will lend an aura of professionalism to you that often pays off literally in terms of increased sales and profits. The bottom line is that incorporating may be a wise investment in the area of intangible business assets, in addition to any other benefits realized.

Capitalizing the Corporation; Charitable Contributions
Two other areas unique to corporations are the special means at their disposal for raising money and their ability to deduct charitable contributions.

A closely held corporation can, of course, issue and sell additional shares of stock at any time in order to raise more capital. If your corporation proves very successful in the market place, then at some point you may also consider "going public." A public offering of stock can often provide

---

[11] Illinois law does not legally require you to use a seal, but traditionally corporations do use one to impress their stock certificates and corporate business documents. You will be asked for its impress on formal business agreements, such as the application for a bank loan or the application to open a corporate bank account. Seals can be ordered from some stationery stores. The P. Gaines Co. also includes a seal custom engraved with your business name as part of the complete corporate

outfit it provides as a courtesy to its customers. See the order form in the back of this book.

hundreds of thousands or even millions of dollars in capital to growing corporations eager for expansion. If your stock is publicly traded, furthermore, you also have other avenues of financing open to you, through the issuance of corporate bonds (notes secured by company assets) and debentures (unsecured notes).

Corporations, unlike sole proprietors and partnerships, also have the right to deduct charitable contributions up to 10 percent of income each year (larger contributions can be carried over to future years and deducted from income). If you have a particular cause you want to support, then your corporation provides you an ideal tax-free means of doing so!

Summary: Major Advantages and Disadvantages of Incorporating

Advantages

1. One of the greatest advantages of the corporate form is that the owner(s) of the corporation is (are) not personally liable for the debts of the corporation (taking into account the exceptions noted—malpractice on the part of incorporated professionals, directorial fraud, malfeasance, or breach of fiduciary duty, loyalty, and care; unpaid taxes; and loans secured by personal assets).

2. The corporation as a tax shelter offers a number of tax-saving advantages not available to the sole proprietor or partnership, including lower tax brackets,[12] tax-free income in the form of medical reimbursements, pension and profit-sharing plans, "free" life, accident, and health insurance, tuition reimbursement plans paying up to $5,250 per employee for either work-related or non-work-related educational expenses, group legal services plans paying up to $70 per employee annually, and plans providing employees with dependent care assistance worth up to $5,000 per year tax-free.

3. The perpetual existence of the corporate entity gives it increased stability, enabling it to withstand changes in ownership or management.

4. Subject to certain limitations, a corporation may own shares in other corporations and receive dividends, 70 percent of which are tax-free. With a 20 percent or larger

---

[12] Although corporate income above $75,000 is taxed at the rate of 34 percent, the first $50,000 of that income is taxed at only 15 percent, and the next $25,000 at 25 percent.

ownership stake, the tax-free payback increases to 80 percent.

5. The shareholder(s)-owner(s) of a corporation can operate with all the benefits of a corporation but be taxed at personal income tax rates if this proves advantageous, as in the case of certain closely held family corporations (see Chapter 8, "The S Corporation").

6. The capital of the corporation can be increased with relative ease by issuing and selling to oneself or to other investors additional shares of stock. Corporations also have the option of making a public offering of stock and of raising capital through the issuance of corporate bonds and debentures.

7. As an employee, you can receive loans from your corporation.

8. The corporate image itself can be a valuable intangible business asset in your dealing with clients, employees, creditors, and banks.

9. Individuals receiving Social Security payments and still working can use incorporation to escape the limits on earned income. In 2003, those 62 to 64 years of age can earn only $11,520 without penalty. The Social Security Administration will take $1 for each $2 earned above this limit. That amounts to a whopping 50 percent income tax rate on those earnings on top of the regular federal and state income taxes. This amount of $11,520 is indexed for inflation and rises each year. Furthermore, in the year you turn 65 you can currently earn up to $30,720 without penalty. The good news is that the limits on earned income for those receiving Social Security benefits between the ages of 65 and 69 have been abolished. By paying yourself no more than the limit on earned income and retaining the balance in the corporation, you would be able to withdraw the remaining income at age 65 when the limits on earned income no longer apply.

10. Under current law, one can use an S corporation to incorporate a stock portfolio or other passive income.

11. One surprising advantage of the corporate form: chances of an IRS audit are substantially less. You are three times more likely to be audited by the IRS if you are a sole proprietor with more than $100,000 in annual income than if you are operating as a corporation with assets under $250,000.

Disadvantages

1. One small disadvantage of incorporation is the added expense you will pay in terms of fees, but these are extremely reasonable in Illinois (some of the lowest in the country): the one-time minimum incorporation fee of $75, plus the initial minimum franchise tax of $25, for a total of $100 for profit corporations, and an annual report of continued existence, whose minimum filing fee totals $50.

2. In order to use small claims courts in many states, corporations (unlike individuals, sole proprietors, and partnerships) must be represented by an attorney. This is a decided disadvantage for the incorporated small business person who uses small claims court to collect unpaid bills. In Illinois, the law has been liberalized to allow a corporate officer to represent the corporation in court. Attorneys are not allowed to appear in small claims court. This "disadvantage" turns out to be an advantage instead, because the legislature is attuned to the unique needs of the small, incorporated business person in Illinois.

3. Unless your net taxable business earnings are at least $25,000, there may not be substantial tax advantages to incorporating (although other advantages, such as limitation of personal liability, will still hold). As a general rule, the higher your income, the more tax savings you will realize and the more fringe benefits you will be able to take advantage of as a corporation.

4. If you incorporate, you will pay more Social Security taxes than you would as a self-employed person (approximately 2 percent more, at present). On the plus side, these extra taxes are fully deductible by the corporation as a business expense, but not by the self-employed individual. (Since 1990, however, when the self-employment rate and the combined employer-employee corporate rate of Social Security and Medicare tax each equalled 15.3 percent, self-employers have been able to deduct half their self-employment tax as a business expense.)

The current higher rate of Social Security tax paid by corporations will not result in any extra Social Security benefits when you retire. In the case of a wife working for the incorporated business, the couple's combined Social Security taxes may seem doubly burdensome. Since a low-income spouse will receive more, upon retirement, from her husband's account than she will from her own account, her Social Security benefits are, in a sense, wasted, although required by law.

In other circumstances, she will stand to benefit, however. In the event of her death, her minor children can collect benefits on her account. She may also choose to retire and start collecting Social Security benefits while her husband continues working. If the marriage does not last 10 years, she cannot draw on benefits from her husband's account, so she will need her own retirement plan. According to one study, the average marriage today lasts only about 9 years, so the additional Social Security tax paid by the corporation on behalf of a working spouse may turn out to be a blessing in disguise.

5. You will be required to pay an unemployment tax to the state and federal governments to cover yourself as an employee of the corporation.

6. The increased paperwork in maintaining the corporate records and in filing two tax returns (individual and corporate) will be another price of doing business as a corporation. Since 1984, most small corporations have been able to file the short-form federal corporate return (Form 1120-A). This simplifies matters somewhat. The state of Illinois also requires the filing of an annual corporate franchise (income) tax return. If you are knowledgeable about tax laws and normally file your own tax returns, you may well be able to continue doing so for your corporation. If not, you will need to hire a tax preparer or accountant to handle the filings.

7. If you are already operating a business as a sole proprietor or as a member of a partnership, you may incur certain relatively minor expenses in notifying the public of your new status as a corporation, such as changing your telephone listings, having new stationery printed, and so on.

8. The fee charged by an attorney for an incorporation averages out to be around $1000. Those willing to invest the time and energy to set up their own corporation, even if they have a lawyer review their incorporation papers, can still save most of these organizational costs. Approximately one-third of all new corporations are formed without a lawyer, so if you decide to go it on your own, you are not alone!

TO INCORPORATE OR NOT . . .

We have given an overview of the corporation as a form of business ownership, in contrast to the sole proprietorship, the partnership, and the limited liability company, and have noted some of the major advantages and disadvantages of incorporating. Subsequent chapters will deal in greater detail with the various topics introduced here. Before reaching a decision in your individual case on whether or not to incorporate, be sure to consider all the pros and cons. Plan to consult an attorney, particularly if there are special aspects to your situation.

Chapter 2. The Illinois Corporation

The first chapter was intended to acquaint you with the operation of corporations in general. In this chapter, we will focus on the Illinois corporation.

Purposes of a Corporation

The Illinois Business Corporation Act defines the types and powers of profit corporations that may be set up in the state and the laws governing their conduct. It is this Act that the following discussion will highlight.

In Article 3 of this Act, the broad range of purposes for which Illinois corporations may be organized is defined as follows:

Corporations for profit may be organized under this Act for any lawful purpose or purposes, except for the purpose of banking or insurance.

This statement does not exclude certain professional corporations—such as those owned and operated by dentists and physicians—from organizing under this section. These types of professional corporations are authorized under another section, Section 3.05. A

separate chapter (Chapter 6) will be devoted to the Illinois Professional Service Corporation.

Two common types of corporations excluded from incorporating under the main section but authorized to incorporate under other statutes will be treated in later chapters of this book. These include the Professional Service Corporation (Chapter 6) and the Not for Profit Corporation (see Chapter 7).

In short, any "lawful" activity may be incorporated in Illinois under the provisions of the Business Corporation Act, with the exceptions noted. Corporations falling under a *special* provision, such as banks and insurance companies as well as not for profits and professional services corporations, shall be organized under that provision. All others are free to organize under the general provisions, as stated above.

In filling out the Articles of Incorporation (see Appendix A in the back of this book), you do not need to describe or specify the type of business you are incorporating.[1] The purpose of the corporation may be simply stated as follows:

The transaction of any or all lawful businesses for which corporations may be organized under the Business Corporation Act.[2]

---

[1] An exception to this rule is the professional service corporation, which requires a specific purpose clause in the Articles of Incorporation, naming the profession to be engaged in and the address from which services will be rendered. Such Chapter 6, "The Illinois Professional Service Corporation."

[2] In the past, several paragraphs were required in the Articles of Incorporation in order to state the exact nature and legal ramifications of each

We will focus on the Illinois for-profit corporation for the remainder of this chapter.

Powers of Profit Corporations

Section 3.10 of the Illinois Business Corporation Act spells out the particular activities that the law authorizes Illinois corporations to engage in. In spite of the pretentiousness of the language, we suggest that you go over this list carefully. This attentive reading will give you an appreciation of the types of power your corporation will enjoy in the event you incorporate your business.

1. To have perpetual existence, unless a limited period of duration is stated in the corporation's Articles of Incorporation.

2. To sue and be sued, complain and defend, in its corporate name.

3. To have, use, and alter at pleasure.a corporate seal. The use of the seal is not mandatory.

4. To purchase, take, receive, lease as leasee, take by gift, legacy, or otherwise acquire, and to own, hold, use, and otherwise deal in and with, any real or personal property, or an interest therein, situated in or out of this State.

5. To sell and convey, mortgage, pledge, lease as lessor, and otherwise dispose of all or any part of its property and assets.

6. To lend money to its directors, officers, employees, and agents.

7. Subject to certain restrictions, to purchase, take, receive, subscribe for, or otherwise acquire, own, hold, vote, use, employ, sell, mortgage, loan, pledge, or otherwise dispose of, and otherwise use and deal in and with, shares or other interests in or obligations of, other domestic or foreign corporations, associations, partnerships, or individuals.

8. To incur liabilities, to borrow money for its corporate purposes at such rate of interest as the corporation may determine without regard to the restrictions of any usury law of this State; to issue its notes, bonds and other obligations by mortgage, pledge, or deed of trust of all or any of its property, franchises, and income; and to make contracts, including contracts of guaranty and suretyship, provided that a corporation may not be organized hereunder for the purpose of insurance.

9. To invest its surplus funds from time to time and to lend money for its corporate purposes, and to take and hold real and personal property as security for the payment of funds so invested or loaned.

10. To conduct its business, carry on its operations, and have offices within and without this State and to exercise in any other state, territory, district, or possession of the United States, or in any foreign country, the powers granted by this Act..

11. To elect or appoint officers, employees, and other agents of the corporation, define their duties, and fix their compensation

12. With certain exceptions in times of national emergencies, to make and alter bylaws not inconsistent with its Articles of Incorporation or with the laws of the State, for the administration and regulation of the affairs of the corporation..

13. To make donations for the public welfare or for charitable, scientific, religious, civic, or educational purposes; to lend money to the

---

particular type of business incorporated. With the present simplified procedure, this detailed description is no longer necessary or advisable.

State or Federal government; and to transact any lawful business in aid of the United Sates.

14. To cease its corporate activities and surrender its corporate franchise.

15. To establish deferred compensation plans, pension plans, profit-sharing plans, share bonus plans, share option plans, and other incentive plans for its directors, officers, and employees, and to make the payments and issue the shares provided for therein.

16. To indemnify its directors, officers, employees, or agents, in accordance with and to the extent permitted by Section 8.75 of the Business Corporation Act.

17. To be a promoter, partner, member, associate, or manager of any partnership, joint venture, or other enterprise.

18. To have and exercise all powers necessary or convenient to effect any or all of the purposes for which the corporation is formed.

Eyes and Ears of the Corporation

Since the corporation is a fictitious person, real people must carry on the actual work of the corporation. These individuals who conduct the business of the corporation fall into four basic categories,[3] according to their roles:

Incorporators
Directors
Officers
Shareholders

Many corporations will also have other employees or workers, in addition to the officers who run the business on a day-to-day basis. In a one-man or one-woman corporation, a single individual will play all these parts. Wanda Gold may wear all the hats at Wanda Gold Enterprises, Inc. In a larger corporation, these jobs will be divided among separate individuals. Even here there is generally some overlapping, particularly between the board of directors and officers of the corporation. At A.T.&T., for example, Robert Allen served for years as both chairman of the board of directors and chief executive officer (president).

---

[3] These categories exist in virtually all corporations, but we are concerned in the following discussion primarily with the specific delimitations of these categories in the Illinois statutes.

Incorporators

The incorporators, also referred to in common parlance as the "promoters"[4] of the corporation, are the persons who sign the Articles of Incorporation and who make practical arrangements to set up the corporation. Such arrangements may include a broad canopy of activities, from drawing up employment contracts and leasing office space to naming the initial board of directors. (It is advisable, for legal reasons, however, to postpone making employment contracts, renting office space, and entering into other types of contractual agreements until after the corporation has been formed.)

Although we have referred to "incorporators," the minimum number of such individuals required by Illinois law is at present only one. Unlike some states, there is a minimum age limit for incorporators in Illinois. Each incorporator is required by law in Illinois to be at least 18 years old.

The incorporator(s) is (are) responsible for raising start-up capital for the corporation. Some states specify a minimum amount of capital that a corporation must raise before commencing business. Illinois, following the trend of other states, such as New York, California, and Ohio, no longer specifies by law a minimum dollar amount as a prerequisite to incorporate.

From a practical standpoint, however, most any business will require working capital. From a legal standpoint, your corporation should have at least enough capital to begin operations and to pay foreseeable, short-range expenses. If not, your "thin" (undercapitalized) corporation may run into legal problems, resulting in your being subjected to personal liability by the courts for the corporation's unpaid debts. If you already have an existing business, then as incorporator you can transfer assets from it in return for shares of stock.[5]

In the event that you are starting your Illinois corporation from scratch, you will need either to provide seed money from your personal funds (a portion of which may be in the form of loans to the corporation) or to find investors to capitalize the corporation in exchange for stock. Later in this chapter we will look at the role of the stockholder, whether that of the incorporator herself or other investors.

Directors

The board of directors (which may consist of a single director in Illinois) oversees the business operations of the corporation. The number of directors shall be fixed by the corporate bylaws, except the number of initial directors shall be fixed by the incorporators in the Articles of Incorporation or at the organizational meeting. If the bylaws do not fix the number of subsequent

---

[4] While most small corporations are formed by individuals, it is important to note that, under Illinois law, a partnership or a corporation (whether domestic or foreign, profit or non-profit) or any other association or legal entity may also act as incorporator of an Illinois corporation

---

[5] See Chapter 5 for specific recommendations on the transfer of assets from an existing business and start-up loans for your corporation.

directors, the number shall be that of the initial board as fixed in the Articles.

The Articles may also provide that there not be a board of directors and that one or more shareholders manage the corporation under a so-called "shareholders' agreement," in accordance with the Illinois Close Corporation Act of 1977. Such small corporations that do not have a board of directors and are managed by one or more shareholders are usually referred to as "close corporations" or "closely held corporations."

The duties of the board of directors ordinarily include making major policy decisions and managing the distribution of money. The board of directors typically decides when and how much the company will pay out in dividends to its stockholders and how much will remain in the company for its capital needs, research and development, and ordinary business expenses.

Directors of Illinois corporations do not have to be of a set age or residents of this state, unless the Articles of Incorporation or bylaws so prescribe. They shall have such qualifications, if any, as are stated in the Articles of Incorporation or the corporate bylaws. It is common practice for directors to serve without pay, since their work is ordinarily performed in order to increase the value of their stock holdings in the corporation. Directors in Illinois do not have to be stockholders, however, so financial compensation (including pension, disability, and death benefits) is permitted by law as long as it is given for real services. In addition,

directorial salaries must be authorized in advance at a meeting of the board of directors, by the affirmative vote of a majority of directors then in office. Directorial salaries may be subject to approval of the shareholders if the Articles of Incorporation or bylaws so provide.

Traditionally, the board of directors meets once a month, although small corporations can often get by with one annual meeting (usually held on the same day as, and immediately after, the annual shareholders' meeting). Of course, special meetings may also be called at any time during the year in order to document a formal resolution, for instance, a director's resolution authorizing a bank loan.

Informal meetings or even phone conferences may also be held to decide a particular issue. In such cases, the directors should sign a written consent setting forth the action so taken and file these consents with the minutes of the directors' meetings.

Special meetings shall be held upon notice as prescribed in the bylaws. A majority of directors is necessary to constitute a quorum for a meeting of directors. The act of a majority of the directors present at the meeting is the act of the board, unless the act of a greater number is required by the Articles of Incorporation, the corporate bylaws, or the Illinois Business Corporation Act. Amendment of the bylaws by the board requires the vote of not less than a majority of the members of the board then in office.

Appendix D contains forms for the Minutes of the First Meeting of the Board of Directors. Recommended instructions for filling out these forms are included in Chapter 5. Even if you are the only director/officer of the corporation, you are required to keep minutes for the first and all subsequent meetings and file them permanently with the corporate records (unless you choose to dispense with the board of directors and state in the Articles of incorporation or the corporate bylaws that the corporation shall be managed under a "close corporation agreement"). The corporate minutes contain vital information about your company regarding annual compensation, the issuance of stock, new or amended corporate bylaws, and the election of officers.

The directors are *always* elected by the stockholders. This election may be a mere formality when the corporation has only one or two stockholders who choose themselves as directors. In a large corporation, this is one of the main functions of the stockholders, to vote for the board of directors.

The Illinois Business Corporation Act provides for a maximum term of three years for directors from the date of election until successors are elected, in the case of corporations with staggered terms (See Section 8.10, subsection e). If the Articles of Incorporation or corporate bylaws do not specify the terms of directors, however, each director shall hold office until the next annual meeting of shareholders and until his or her successor is elected, or until his or her earlier resignation,

removal from office, or death. Since the Illinois statutes do not forbid a director from running for re-election, you may continue to elect the same director(s) year after year. Further discussion of the voting procedures for the election of directors will follow in the section on "Shareholders" below.

Unless otherwise provided by the Articles of Incorporation or corporate bylaws, a director or the entire board may be removed, with or without cause, by vote of the holders of a majority of the shares entitled to vote at an election of directors, subject to the provisions of Section 8.35 of the Business Corporation Act. A 1985 amendment to this act authorizes the Articles of corporations having a board with staggered terms to provide, if desired, that directors may be removed *for cause only.*

A director may resign by written notice to the corporation. The resignation is effective upon its receipt by the corporation or at a later time as set forth in the notice of resignation.

Directors may also adopt a resolution dissolving the corporation in the event of bankruptcy, the expiration of the period of existence of a limited-life corporation specified in its Articles of Incorporation, or the cancellation of the Articles for failure to file annual reports or excise tax returns or pay taxes due, when the corporation has not been reinstated or does not desire to be reinstated.

Officers

The primary officers of a corporation ordinarily consist of a president, a secretary, and a treasurer, and, if desired, a chairman of the board and one or more vice-presidents. Other officers or assistants may also be elected, as needed, as specified in the corporate bylaws.

The officers shall be elected by the board of directors, at such time and in such manner as may be prescribed in the bylaws. None of the officers need be a director, but, in a closely held corporation, some, if not all, of the officers will undoubtedly be chosen from among the directors.

The officers are in charge of running the corporation on a day-to-day basis. Therefore, a large corporation will require many more officers than a small corporation. The exact duties of the officers are either defined in the corporate bylaws or by the board of directors. To avoid confusion, the bylaws should state the officer titles of your corporation as well as their duties, which, of course, may be customized according to the particular needs of your business. Generic descriptions of the usual four—president, vice-president, secretary, and treasurer—are included in the sample bylaws in Appendix B.

Officers in Illinois no longer have to be called by conventional titles. You have the option of designating a "First Potentate" or "Master of the Nether Worlds" instead of a President, for instance, although such unconventional titles may not be advisable for ordinary

businesses. Imagine the response you will get from a stuffy bank vice-president if you go to apply for a loan and present your business card, which reads: John Smith, *Top Dog Extraordinary*, of the Parrot Sales Company.

In Illinois, if the bylaws or Articles of Incorporation so provide, any two or more offices may be held by the same person, without any limitation whatsoever.

An officer elected or appointed shall hold office for the term for which he is elected or appointed and until his successor is elected or appointed and qualified, or until his resignation or removal. Officers are elected in a manner and at a time provided in the bylaws. The sample bylaws in Appendix B specify officer elections by the board of directors, at either an annual meeting or a special meeting.

An officer may be removed by the board of directors, whenever, in its judgment, the best interests of the corporation will be served thereby, but such removal shall be without prejudice to the contract rights, if any, of the person removed. An officer may also resign by written notice to the corporation.

Our friend Wanda as sole director-shareholder, for example, may hold all four offices of president, vice-president, secretary, and treasurer of Wanda Gold Enterprises, Inc. if the bylaws or Articles so allow. If her brother Junior is also willing to serve as an officer, they may decide to divide these four positions between them. Wanda, for instance, can be:

(1) president and vice-president (in theory, although in reality this combination would not be a good choice, since the vice-president normally "substitutes" for the president in his or her absence)
(2) president and treasurer
(3) vice-president and secretary
(4) secretary and treasurer
(5) vice-president and treasurer, or
(6) president and secretary of the corporation

with Junior holding the other two offices remaining in each case. Or Wanda may choose to hold three offices, and Junior one, or vice-versa. If their mother Giesela also wants to be an officer, then the three of them can divide up the four positions any way they choose. There exists a wide range of flexibility in this area.

As in the case of directors, a sole stockholder-director does not have to hold all the offices, unless she chooses to do so. She can find other persons within or outside the family circle to fill additional positions, enlisting relatives, friends, or business contacts as officers. Or you may designate that your corporation will have only one executive office, that of president, which you yourself will fill. If one person holds all the offices of a corporation, the business will usually be organized as a closely held corporation and be so stated in the Articles of Incorporation and/or the bylaws. The share certificates of the corporation must also be designated a "Close Corporation." See Chapter 5 as well as

Appendix E, "Incorporation under a Close Corporation Agreement," for additional information on this point.

As noted above, sample bylaws that define the duties of the main offices of president, vice-president, secretary, and treasurer appear in Appendix B, with the provision that the board may create other offices considered necessary. The president is the chief executive officer who directs the business affairs of the corporation. He or she has the power to "bind" the corporation in contracts and in debt obligations. Other duties, such as the power to hire and fire employees, vary from one corporation to another and should be spelled out in the bylaws.

The vice-president assumes the duties of the president in case of his or her absence or disability and performs other duties as prescribed by the board of directors. Unlike the president, however, he or she does not normally have the power to bind the corporation legally unless authorized to do so in a specific circumstance.

The secretary keeps the minutes of all the meetings of the directors and shareholders and is in charge of the bylaws of the corporation and the share register showing the names and addresses of the shareholders. The secretary also notifies the shareholders and directors of meetings, has charge of the corporate seal, and assumes other duties specified by the president or the board.

The treasurer keeps the account books of the corporation, makes deposits of money, pays creditors, and prepares and presents financial reports on the corporation to the president and the board. The manner and nature of performance of the duties of the corporate officers are subject to the final authority of the directors.

The salaries of the officers are set by the board of directors, subject to approval of the shareholders if the Articles of Incorporation or bylaws so provide. As in the case of the salaries of directors, compensation must be reasonable and given for real services to the corporation. If your business chooses not to pay its stockholder-officers a salary but opts instead to repay their efforts on behalf of the corporation through stock dividends, the bylaws should so state.

Shareholders
Like the limited partners of a partnership agreement, the shareholders of a corporation are under no obligation to the creditors of the corporation or to the corporation itself, beyond paying the full amount due for the shares they purchase. If Wanda Gold is the sole shareholder of her company, as shareholder she has no legal obligation to the corporation after paying for her stock. It is in her additional role as director and officer that she owes the corporation a fiduciary duty. That is, she must look out for the best interests of the corporation, act honestly in her business dealings with it, give it the right of first refusal, and so on.

Besides providing capital and thus quite literally owning the corporation, the shareholders have several other functions as well. Most importantly, as already noted, they vote for the board of directors.

Traditionally, Illinois has been one of the few states that, in the past, permitted every share of every class of stock automatically to receive one vote. The 1983 amendment to the Business Corporation Act authorizes any corporation to abolish cumulative voting and to create non-voting stock, if desired. Except as otherwise provided in the Articles of Incorporation, directors shall be elected by a plurality of votes cast at an election.

Under democratic procedure, we might expect each outstanding share of the corporation to be entitled to one vote. In the case of the election of directors, this basic principle is procedurally altered in a certain way through what is known as "cumulative voting." In Illinois, cumulative voting is in effect unless specifically limited or eliminated by the Articles of Incorporation. Under cumulative voting procedures, each share still receives one vote, but the shareholder has the right to cumulate such voting power as he possesses and to give one directorial candidate as many votes as the number of directors to be elected multiplied by the number of his shares equals, or to divide his votes on the same principle between two or more candidates as he so desires. The purpose of cumulative voting is to protect the interests of minority stockholders. An example will show how it works.

Take the case of Joe Stockholder, who owns 20 shares of stock in Wonder

Widgets, Inc., a closely held Illinois corporation that presently has three positions on the board of directors to fill. If cumulative voting procedures are in effect, Joe will have 60 votes to cast in whatever manner he wishes. If Mary Public, the only other stockholder in the same corporation, owns 30 shares, her total voting power will amount to 90 votes. Even though Joe is a minority shareholder, by cumulating all of his 60 votes for one candidate, he has the ability to elect at least one representative to the board of directors, while Mary has sufficient voting power to elect the other two. Without cumulative voting, however, Joe would receive *no* representation on the board, since Mary would always be able to outvote him under normal voting procedures. Joe does not *have* to pool all his votes behind one candidate. He can use his votes in whatever combination he desires. But only by voting all his shares for one candidate can he be certain of electing his own man (or woman!) to the board. Cumulative voting is only operable for the election of directors to the board. Cumulative voting *cannot* be employed for other matters brought before the shareholders for a vote.

Shareholders also have certain other rights defined by the Business Corporation Act. Shareholders' approval is required for mergers and consolidations of the corporation with ·another and for the amendment of the Articles of Incorporation. In addition, voluntary dissolution of the corporation may be elected by vote of the shareholders. Instead of the two-thirds vote of shareholders formerly required

to effect such changes, an Illinois corporation may now provide in its Articles for a smaller or larger vote requirement than two-thirds (but not less than a majority of the outstanding shares entitled to vote).

Just as the shareholders participate in the profits of the corporation through dividends, so too would they share in the distribution of the assets of the corporation upon voluntary or involuntary dissolution.

Sale of Stock

The Illinois Business Corporation Act specifies that corporate stock may be paid, in whole or in part, in money or in other property, tangible or intangible, or in labor or services performed or to be performed for the corporation[6] for its benefit or in its organization or reorganization. This initial amount of payment for stock can be in cash or in other assets, including equipment (for example, a truck, restaurant fixtures, tables and chairs), inventories, accounts receivable, etc. Thus you have wide

---

[6] In the past, promissory notes were *not* allowed as payment for shares of stock. The restriction against the issuance of promissory notes has been eliminated. Now you can pay for shares of stock with the *promise* of payment of money or *future* services to the corporation.

leeway in how you capitalize the corporation.

If you as sole owner of the business have capital assets consisting of any combination of cash and/or property, then you can exchange all, or a portion of, these assets for stock to begin business as a corporation. During the course of your operation as a corporation, you may take part of your compensation for actual work performed in the form of additional shares of stock. This is a common practice of many business executives of both small and large corporations, enabling them frequently to amass large stock portfolios.

On the Illinois Articles of Incorporation form, you will be asked to specify the type of stock to be issued, whether common or preferred, and its par value, if any.

A little background information may prove helpful about this point, since the records of the corporation and its stock certificates would ordinarily indicate whether the stock of the corporation has par value or not.

The par value of a preferred stock represents the dollar value on which the stock's dividend is based. For instance, a 10 percent preferred, $20 par value stock would pay an annual dividend of $2.00 per share (10 percent of $20). Most small corporations do not issue preferred stock, however.

In regard to common stock, par value is an arbitrary amount that may be assigned to each share of a company's common stock under the company's

charter issued by the state when it incorporates. It is primarily a bookkeeping device. Stock with a par value of $10 cannot be sold for less than its face value, whereas no-par value stock can be sold at any value set by the board of directors or shareholders.

It is ordinarily simpler for most small corporations to issue common, no par-value stock, due to the greater leeway in allocating funds within the corporation from the sale of this type of stock.[7]

The Illinois Articles of Incorporation form asks the incorporator(s) to specify the number of shares of stock authorized. Theoretically, this number can be almost anything, for instance, from 1 to 100,000 shares of stock might be authorized and issued. In practice, however, we recommend the following guidelines:

(1) The number of authorized shares should be large.
(2) The number of authorized shares should be greater than the number actually issued.
(3) The number of shares authorized and issued should ideally be divisible by as many numbers as possible.[8]

---

[7] In the case of par value stock, if the face value is $10 and the stock sells for $12, $10 of every $12 received as payment must go into the capital reserves; the $2 excess constitutes capital surplus. In the case of no-par value stock, gains from its sale may be allocated between stated capital and capital surplus in any proportion decided by the board.
[8] This precaution may keep you from having to deal with fractional shares later on.

Either 3,000 or 6,000 shares might be a good choice for the number of authorized shares, since both of these numbers are relatively large and divisible by 2,3,4,5, and 6. If you issued only 300 no-par value shares of the authorized number for a consideration of $9,000, for example, you would later be able to make additional issues of shares without further report to the Secretary of State.[9] In this way, you can increase the capital of your corporation in the future if need be by issuing and buying additional shares of stock yourself. Or you may decide to sell shares to other investors, reward an employee with a gift of stock, or transfer part of the ownership of the company to other family members through donations of stock.

The Illinois Business Corporation Act permits corporations to have different classes of stock, such as voting and nonvoting. These rights and limitations must be spelled out in the Articles of Incorporation. Otherwise, every share of stock is entitled to vote. At one time in the past, you were not allowed under federal law to adopt Subchapter S status, discussed in Chapter 8, if your corporation had both voting and nonvoting stock. The Subchapter S Revision Act of 1982 eliminated this restriction, however.

Some family corporations wishing to keep control of the corporation within the hands of several family members while giving other family members (say, their children or retired parents) dividend-paying shares of stock may want to devise voting and nonvoting classes of stock. Legal counsel is highly advisable in such a case.

---

[9] No further report (and filing expense) would be required as long as you did not wish to issue more shares than the number authorized in the original Articles. It pays to plan ahead. If you do later wish to authorize additional shares, a certificate of amendment to the Articles must be filed, along with a filing fee plus a franchise fee that depends on the value of additional shares authorized.

Chapter 3. Should I Form a Delaware Corporation?

There are a number of books on the market today that advocate forming a Delaware corporation, regardless of which state you live and do business in. These books are invariably written and published by Delaware companies that want to sell you their services as "registered agents."[1]

Nevada, like Delaware, is another state that actively courts out-of-state businesses to incorporate within its borders. There is nothing illegal about forming a Delaware or Nevada corporation, even if you are doing business exclusively in Illinois. Whether it is advisable is another question. An objective look at the issue of whether a Delaware corporation can

be recommended for the Illinois small business person follows.

In the past, certain businesses in Illinois and other states did find it advantageous to incorporate out of state because of tax and legal loopholes. All states, including Illinois, have now closed these loopholes. You cannot avoid Illinois taxes and fees by forming a Delaware corporation.

Those publications that recommend Delaware corporations sometimes imply that persons residing in other states with minimum capitalization requirements can bypass these requirements by incorporating in Delaware. Illinois, like Delaware, does not fix by law a specific minimum capitalization for new corporations. You don't have to ante up a specific amount of money to launch your new Illinois corporation, in other words. Delaware corporations, therefore, do not hold an advantage over Illinois ones in regard to minimum capitalization requirements.

In reality, no one starts a corporation without any capital whatsoever. This is a very risky proposition, from a financial and a legal standpoint. (See the discussion of "thin" corporations in the previous chapter.) Even in states with minimum capital requirements (generally a $500 or $1,000 minimum), this minimum is certainly a "bare" minimum. Almost all businesses would require more than this sum as start-up working capital.

One conceivable case in which you might choose to form an out-of-state corporation is if you are under 18 years

---

[1] If you form a Delaware corporation but your business is located in another state, you would require a registered agent with a Delaware mailing address who would forward your Delaware Articles of Incorporation, annual reports, and other official papers from the state of Delaware to you.

of age, since Illinois requires that incorporators be at least 18 years old. Currently, some 30 states do have such an age requirement, while several others specify only that the incorporator must be "capable to contract."

Although Illinois is one of these states that does have a minimum age requirement for incorporators, the incorporator(s) does (do) not have to be (a) stockholder(s). Therefore, if you are under 18 years of age, you can have an adult file the incorporation papers for you (a lawyer, parent, or friend, for example). This is a perfectly acceptable procedure that allows you to be sole stockholder of an Illinois corporation if you so choose even if you are legally a minor.

In summary, we began by observing that in the past it was advantageous for some Illinois businesses to incorporate out of state. Most frequently, these out-of-state corporations were formed in Delaware, because of the simplicity of the corporate laws and low fees in that state. Owing to changes in the laws governing foreign corporations (corporations operating in one state but domiciled in another), there exist very few cases where a Delaware corporation would now benefit an Illinois business person.

The only possible exceptions to this general rule are very large, publicly traded corporations that operate interstate or internationally. These types of corporations may gain certain technical advantages in such areas as voting rights by incorporating in Delaware. Some companies initially incorporate or later re-incorporate in Delaware because Delaware corporate regulations sometimes make it easier for a company to defend against unwanted takeovers, for example. This is obviously not a problem that small, privately held Illinois corporations have to worry about. For the Illinois business person with capitalization under $500,000, a Delaware corporation is *not* recommended.

The distinct disadvantage of a Delaware corporation is that it will cost you additional, unnecessary time and expense, if you are doing business in Illinois (not Delaware). If you form a Delaware corporation, you will have to register in Illinois as a foreign corporation, as noted above. As a foreign corporation, you will pay the same initial filing and franchise fees as an Illinois domestic corporation and the same amount of annual tax on income and assets.

Don't forget that, in addition, you will have to pay Delaware license or filing fees and franchise taxes as well. These are not just extra, one-time expenses. You will be paying these double franchise taxes annually as long as you continue to operate under the guise of a Delaware corporation. Unless you plan to open an office in Delaware, you will also have to hire a registered agent to provide you with a Delaware mailing address (required by law for foreign corporations doing business in the state). In general, those who advocate Delaware corporations for anyone and everyone are putting a large number of individuals to additional trouble and expense, with no offsetting advantage.

Also, if you form a Delaware corporation and fail to register as a foreign corporation with the Illinois Secretary of State, you may be denied the use of the court system of this state for the purpose of initiating civil actions and will be personally liable for business debts and lawsuits. If you later decide to pay the fees in order to use the courts (or are detected and made to pay), you will owe all past due filing fees and franchise taxes, plus penalties.

In addition to any other liabilities imposed by law, a foreign corporation conducting affairs in the state without a certificate of authority will be liable for a penalty of either 10 percent of the filing fees, license fees and franchise taxes owed or $200 plus $5 for each month in which it has continued to transact business in the state without a certificate of authority, whichever penalty is greater. All amounts due shall be recovered with costs in an action prosecuted by the Attorney General.

In short, unless you are actually planning to conduct your business in another state, it is easier, cheaper, and smarter for you to incorporate in Illinois.

Chapter 4. Taxes and the Corporation as a Tax Shelter

The tax man cometh, not only for you and me personally but also for corporations. In this chapter, we will consider the various taxes paid by Illinois corporations as well as some of the main ways of minimizing taxes through the corporate form of business ownership. Clearly, the corporation is often the most advantageous type of business when it comes to minimizing taxes. When you incorporate, your salary is tax-deductible, your medical coverage (including insurance premiums) is deductible, your disability insurance premium is deductible, most of your life insurance premium is deductible, and practically all other business-related expenses are deductible.

Illinois State Taxes

Corporate Franchise Tax and Annual Report

Every domestic and foreign corporation in Illinois operating for profit is subject to a franchise tax. The annual franchise tax is computed at the rate of $1/10^{th}$ of 1 percent, with a minimum fee of $25.

The *initial* franchise tax at the time of incorporation of your business is assessed at the rate of $15/100^{th}$ of 1 percent of paid-in capital ($1.50 per $1,000, with a minimum tax of $25 and a maximum of $1,000,000). If your stated capital at the time of incorporation is from $0 to $16,667, your initial franchise fee will be $25. If your stated capital is over $16,667 at the time of incorporation, your initial franchise tax will be more than the minimum, computed at the above rate. A corporation with $30,000 in capital, for example, will pay an initial franchise tax of $45. In Chapter 5 under "Articles if Incorporation," we will consider in greater detail the fees which all new corporations must pay, including the franchise tax.

Corporations organized after December 31, 1982 must file once a year with the Secretary of State and pay both an annual filing fee of $25 and an annual franchise tax ($25 for many small corporations). A total of $50 will be owed annually to the state of Illinois by the typical smaller corporation, in other words. This payment, along with the annual report, which asks you to verify and update information about company officers' and directors' names and addresses, new stock issuances, and increases in stated capital of the corporation is due before the first day of the anniversary month of the formation of the corporation. If you incorporated your business in May of 1994, for instance, your annual franchise tax, filing fee and annual report would be due by April 30 of each successive year.[1] Failure to file the annual report and pay the annual franchise tax and filing fee will result in dissolution of your corporation by the Secretary of State.

State Corporate Tax
The Illinois state corporate tax rate currently is 7.3 percent of income. This includes the 4.8 percent corporate rate per se, plus the 2.5 percent so-called "replacement tax." This is a middle of the range corporate rate, compared to other states. The Illinois corporate income tax return is Form IL-1120, which all profit corporations except those with Subchapter S status must file annually. Subchapter S corporations file Form IL-1120ST and currently pay a tax rate of 1.5 percent of net income (See Chapter 8, "The Subchapter S Corporation").

State Sales Tax
Both incorporated and unincorporated Illinois businesses are required to pay sales taxes to the state, collected on retail sales. It is actually the consumer, not the business, who pays these taxes,

but you as a business owner-operator are responsible for collecting the taxes in an orderly fashion and remitting them to the state at regular intervals. The Illinois sales tax rate is currently 6.25 percent on all merchandise except qualifying food, drugs, and medical appliances, which are taxed at 1 percent. Depending on the location of your business, there may be additional add-ons to this basic rate. A business in Oak Park, Illinois, for example, currently has a total Illinois sales tax rate of 8.75 percent, consisting of the base rate of 6.25 percent, plus an additional RTA tax and county home rule tax.

Individual State Income Tax
Any profits distributed to individual shareholders during the year as dividends must be reported on the state personal income tax returns of the recipients. These dividends are taxed at the rate of all personal income in Illinois, presently a flat rate of 3 percent. This tax rate is subject to certain tax credits, including a property tax credit, a retirement and social security income credit, a military pay credit, and an income from U.S. government obligations credit.

Since dividends are taxed at both the corporate and individual level, this results in the famous so-called "double taxation" of corporations. You will want to take this fact into consideration when deciding if and when and how much in dividends to pay the stockholder(s) of the corporation. For most small corporations, double taxation is not a worry, since dividends

---

[1] Each corporation should automatically receive its annual report form and notification of fees owed several months in advance of the due date each year.

do not have to be paid at all, unless the corporation accumulates in excess of $250,000 in assets. Most small corporations will pay out almost all their earnings in salaries and fringe benefits, and will pay no dividends at all. Such a typical situation does not result in any double taxation.

It is usually preferable to take money out of your corporation in ways other than paying dividends, as long as you are not violating the law. More will be said about this issue later in this chapter. Under certain circumstances, you will be required to issue dividends. The IRS has set a ceiling on the amount of money that can accumulate in the company at lower corporate tax rates without being distributed as dividends.

For professional service corporations, such as the health professions and engineering, the limit on accumulated earnings is currently $150,000. For other types of corporations, the limit is set at $250,000. Certain exceptions, such as the need to accumulate additional capital to expand your business or purchase another, are allowed.

A hefty tax penalty is imposed on businesses that exceed their capital accumulations limit without any justification. The corporate minutes of meetings will normally lay the groundwork of plans for expansion, contingency funding, and similar rationales for accumulating capital in excess of the normal limits set by the IRS. The problem for many corporations will be in simply reaching these limits, not in exceeding them!

The legal power to declare dividends rests solely with the board of directors, subject to Illinois laws. In some cases defined by the Illinois statutes, a corporation is not permitted to pay dividends.

Basically, dividends cannot be declared or paid at a time when the corporation is insolvent or when the payment of dividends would make the corporation insolvent or reduce its net assets to less than zero or when the payment of dividends would be contrary to any restriction contained in the Articles of Incorporation. If your corporation will have to pay large dividends to its shareholders on a regular basis, you may consider electing Subchapter S corporate status (See Chapter 8, "The Subchapter S Corporation") under certain circumstances.

Federal Taxes

Corporate Income Tax
As pointed out previously, the federal corporate tax rate is a flat percentage of profits. The multi-tiered system of rates is shown in the following table:

Taxable Income	Rate of Tax
First $50,000	15%
Next $25,000	25%
Next $25,000	34%
$100,000-335,000	39%
Over $335,000	34%

Note that an additional 5 percent tax, up to $11,750, is imposed on corporate taxable income over $100,000 but less than $335,000 (corporations with taxable income of at least $335,000 pay a flat rate of 34 percent).

The Clinton tax act (Omnibus Budget Reconciliation Act of 1993) raised the top corporate rate from 34% to 35%, but this increase affects only businesses with more than $10 million in taxable income.

The regular corporate income tax return is Form 1120. All profit corporations, except those with Subchapter S status (who file Form 1120S), in the past have had to file this return annually by March 15, unless an automatic six-month extension is requested. A simplified corporate form has been available since 1985, Form 1120-A (a corporate "short" form, in other words). All corporations meeting the following requirements can file this two-page return:

(1) Gross receipts, total income, and total assets are each less than $250,000
(2) Any dividend income comes from domestic corporations, qualifies for the 70 percent deduction, and is not from debt-financed securities
(3) It has no nonrefundable tax credits other than the general business credit and the credit for prior year minimum tax
(4) The corporation has no ownership in a foreign corporation nor do foreign owners hold 50 percent or more of its own stock
(5) It is not a member of a controlled group of corporations, a member of a group filing a consolidated return, or a personal holding company
(6) It is not in dissolution or liquidation, nor is it filing its final tax return
(7) It is not a Subchapter S corporation or certain other corporations required to file specialized returns, such as farmers cooperatives, political organizations, condominium associations, and real estate investment trusts

(8) It is not subject to environmental tax under section 59A or to liability for interest relating to certain installment sales

Most small corporations will meet all of these tests, and will find their paperwork greatly reduced by using the short form.

Individual Federal Income Tax
Like the state of Illinois, the federal government also taxes corporate profits paid out to individual shareholders as dividends. These dividends will be shown on each shareholder's Form 1040 as income and will be taxed at the individual's personal income tax rate.

To escape the double taxation referred to above, you may want to retain the balance of the profits in the corporation as long as you do not exceed the ceiling on accumulated earnings. There are many other ways of taking money out of the corporation tax-free, some of which will be discussed below. If your corporation is very profitable or is overcapitalized in the beginning, however, you may eventually have no choice but to distribute a substantial part of the profits as dividends and pay taxes owed. Otherwise, you will be subject to the IRS "accumulated earnings penalty."

Another alternative that avoids double taxation and is often advisable for small, closely held corporations that must pay large dividends regularly is the formation of a Subchapter S corporation (see Chapter 8).

Tax Implications of Employee Compensation and Other Benefits

Salaries

The corporation may deduct on its corporate income tax return as ordinary expenses all amounts paid to employees as salaries. Such salaries must be reasonable and paid for actual services rendered to the corporation.

In this regard, putting family members on the payroll helps to keep income of your business within the family. If family members who draw a salary are not performing duties commensurate with their pay, however, you may have to answer to the IRS. The tax code permits deductions only for "reasonable compensation." This requirement prevents corporations from passing unreasonably large sums of tax-free money to its employee(s).[2] The IRS disallows inflated salaries to be deducted, treating the excess instead as disguised dividends.

It will be up to you to prove that the amount of salary of each employee is "reasonable" in terms of duties, qualifications, and skills of the employee, the complexity of the work performed, the size and profitability of your business, the standard of living in your locality, and the salaries of similar employees in similar businesses.

The IRS also considers the relation of the salary of the owner-employee to other key employees; the larger the salary of other key employees, the larger the salary that can be justified for an owner working full time for the business. In general, more sizeable salaries can also be justified for persons who perform multiple executive roles and for those who head highly profitable companies. For such an owner who is by and large responsible for the success of the business, a salary consisting of 50 percent of pretax profits is not unusual.

Somewhere down the road, if you have a very profitable corporation and plan to increase your and other key employees' salaries drastically, you will need to exercise prudence and care, laying the proper groundwork. Salaries should be set early in the year by the board of directors and be tied directly to individual performance and productivity. You may be able to justify paying yourself a salary of, say, $500,000 or even more a year, given your investment of time and money in the business, but be prepared to argue your case.

The IRS often routinely challenges large salaries of one-owner and other closely held or family-run corporations, but its rulings are frequently reversed by the Tax Courts. Judges have ruled $1 million to be reasonable compensation in some cases, but $70 thousand too much in others.

---

[2] The employee is taxed on the salary at his or her individual tax rate, of course, but the corporation can write off the entire amount as a tax deduction. Dividends paid out are likewise taxed to the individual at personal income tax rates, but *cannot* at present be deducted by the corporation as a business expense. In other words, since dividends come out of after-tax earnings, they prove much more costly to the corporation.

In order to help build a case in justifying your salary, you should keep a log of all your business meetings and other professional activities. You might also want to maintain a clipping file of help wanted ads for positions similar to yours that specify a salary. Growth Resources, Inc., a Peabody, Mass. Company which publishes an annual executive compensation report based on a poll of small and medium-sized companies, is another good source of comparative salary data.

Geneva Cos., a financial-services concern in Irvine, California, has studied 2,500 closely held corporations' compensations by industry group. This data reveals a current median compensation for small business owners of $215,460 in businesses with annual revenues between $1 million and $100,000 million. Most highly paid were the owners of primary metal industries ($357,000 a year), while owners of garden and building materials supplies ranked last, with an average compensation of $161,280. "Compensation" in this survey included salary and benefits; salary itself amounted to approximately 78 percent of compensation.[3]

Another possible move is to approve a resolution at a directors' meeting and record it in the minutes covering the contingency of an IRS challenge. The resolution would state that in the event the IRS rules officer salaries to be excessive, the officers in question can

pay back the excess amount to the corporation; further, that the amount returned will be treated as a loan to the employees, for tax purposes.

When you are paying yourself such a sizeable salary as to need to consider such techniques, then expert legal advice would, of course, be called for. It is also permissible to take a larger salary in more profitable years to make up for a smaller salary in leaner years, but, again, the corporate minutes should state that the salary for a particular year in question is above or below average, owing to the financial state of the business.

In general, you should avoid paying large lump-sum bonuses at the end of the year to yourself or other employees. Such bonuses look suspiciously like dividends to the IRS and may be treated as such for tax purposes, since they are paid after the company's earnings for the year are already known. In all tax matters, remember that the success of your claims before the IRS will depend primarily upon the degree of formality you have exercised in your business dealings and the reasonableness of your actions.

---

[3] This survey was done some 14 years ago and has not been updated. We have consequently revised each of the salary figures from the original survey upwards by 25 percent.

Tax-free Pension and Profit-sharing Plans

There exist two basic types of pension plans available to businesses: (1) defined contribution plans and (2) defined benefit plans.[4] The former is much simpler to administer, because it limits the amount of actual contributions to a set dollar amount or a percentage of earnings. Under the 2001 Tax Act, a corporation can make tax-free payments to a defined contribution fund up to the lesser of (a) 25 percent of each employee's annual compensation or (b) $40,000.[5] The amount of money available to the employee during retirement under this arrangement will depend entirely upon the return on pension fund investments.

The second type of pension plan, the defined benefit plan, is more complicated to administer because it pays the retiree a specified amount during retirement. The actual dollar amount of contributions permitted each year can only be determined by an actuary. The 2001 Tax Act permits corporations to set aside sufficient funds in a defined benefit plan to fund a straight life annuity to the employee on retirement equal to the lesser of: (a) $160,000 payout per year[6] or (b) 100 percent of the participant's average compensation for his highest three years. If you choose a defined benefit

plan through an insurance company or a bank, it should do all the actuary work and present you with an IRS-approved master plan that you can adopt for your company.

Both types of plan provide tax-deferred benefits to the employee(s), since the funds are allowed to accumulate tax-free until withdrawal, at which time the employee is likely to be in a lower tax bracket. Since these contributions are completely deductible by the corporation as a business expense, they thereby lower the taxable income of the corporation as well. If the corporation is dissolved, the pension funds can be rolled over tax-free into IRS accounts for its employees.

One very important aspect of corporate pension plan set-asides is that such plans cannot discriminate in the owner-employee's favor. If yours is a one-owner corporation, there appears to be no question of discrimination. There are certain precautions that must be taken in such a case of the one employee who is the sole stockholder.

In addition to being a bona fide plan and meeting the usual requirements, the plan also must provide for coverage of additional employees if and when they are hired. If you company has other employees, you will normally be required to cover them in your benefit plan as well as yourself. You may very well desire to include other employees in your retirement plan as part of your overall employee compensation package.

---

[4] Legal changes have placed retirement plans for unincorporated businesses more on a par with those available to corporations, but some advantages still remain for corporate plans in the case of defined benefit plans.

[5] Down from the maximum allowable contribution per employee of $45,475 in 1982.

[6] To qualify, the plan must be amended to reflect the 2001 law changes.

There exist certain cases in which employees can be excluded from coverage if you so wish. If your corporation hires "independent contractors," then not only will you not have to cover them in your pension or profit-sharing plans (since they are not considered employees), but you will also not have to withhold taxes from their salary or pay their Social Security deductions. Part-time employees who work less than 1,000 hours a year and those under the age of 21 can generally also be excluded from coverage. If you do wish to set up a corporate pension fund, particularly of the defined benefit type, you may need to see a tax consultant in order to insure favorable tax treatment and legality of this and other corporate perks for employees.

Another angle that you should be aware of is the fact that you can, in certain circumstances, act as trustee of your own corporate pension plan, enabling you to lend money from the benefit fund to yourself. As long as your company approves, furthermore, any of the participants in its pension or other deferred compensation plans can borrow a portion of their contributions back.

The 1982 Tax Act has set limits on these loans, however, because of past abuses in which certain individuals were borrowing the full amount of their tax-deductible retirement contributions. Under the new provisions of the law, the maximum amount you can borrow is $50,000 or half your vested money in the plan, whichever is less.

You are allowed to borrow up to $10,000, however, even if that is more than half the amount you have vested. A further stipulation is that a loan must be repaid within five years, unless it is used to buy, build, or refurbish your principal residence. Terms for such home loans range from ten to 25 years.

SEPs
Another pension option especially attractive for the small business owner merits a separate discussion of its own. Simplified Employee Pensions (SEPs for short) offer a relatively new, hassle-free form of retirement plan for **all** types of businesses, whether corporations, partnerships, sole proprietors, or member-managers of a limited liability company. Unlike other types of corporate pension plans, SEPs entail no administrative expense and no burdensome paperwork.

For businesses with very limited resources, SEPs are ideal retirement vehicles because of the ease of setting them up and the benefits they provide, which compares favorably with other types of defined contribution corporate pension plans. They have a $30,000 annual limit or 15 percent of compensation, whichever is less. They offer flexible funding. They also provide another advantage: they can be integrated with Social Security. Most importantly, you do not have to contribute to the plan in those years you can't or choose not to do so.

SEPs for the Masses

The P. Gaines Co. publishes a book about SEPs, **Five Easy Steps to Setting Up an IRS-Approved Retirement Plan for Your Small Business (Incorporated or Unincorporated), With Forms***. Its easy-to-read text, laced with humorous illustrations, explains how any business that is even modestly profitable can establish a SEP immediately. It walks the reader through the five steps for setting up a SEP and includes all needed forms in a tear-out format. See the order form in the back of this book.*

Medical Reimbursement Plans
Corporate employees, their spouses, and dependents can also be covered with a medical reimbursement plan that pays the cost of medical expenses and drugs. All such corporate medical reimbursements are tax-deductible by the corporation as an ordinary business expense and are passed tax-free to the individuals receiving them.[7] Although referred to as "reimbursement plans" by the IRS, your corporation can pay your medical bills and that of your family directly instead of reimbursing you afterward.

In a small or one-owner corporation, there is no reason why your corporation should not pay 100 percent of your and your family's medical expenses not covered by other insurance, provided there are sufficient funds to do so. Again, be sure to consult a tax adviser who specializes in this area to assure favorable tax treatment of the plan. In a larger corporation, it may be necessary to set a ceiling on the actual dollar amount paid out per employee each year.

A model medical reimbursement plan that you may adopt for use by your corporation is included in Appendix E. *This model plan provides for the payment of all medical bills, including premiums for accident and health insurance.*[8]

This coverage, like that of medical and dental expenses and drugs, may be extended to the spouses and dependents as well as the employees themselves. Accident and health insurance coverage does not have to be part of a group plan such as those offered by Blue Cross. You can choose your own plan and have the corporation pay for it.

---

[7] Whereas the corporation can deduct the total amount spent for medical and dental expenses for its employees, the individual taxpayer, as noted in Chapter 1, can deduct only that portion of expenses exceeding 7.5 percent of adjusted gross income.

[8] Unincorporated business owners, whether sole proprietors or partnerships, are now allowed to deduct 100 percent of their health insurance premiums paid for themselves and their spouses and dependents for tax year 2002 and thereafter. Both medical and dental health insurance premiums may be deducted, as well as long-term care insurance premiums. If there are other employees of the business besides the owner, they too must be provided coverage. If an individual owner is eligible to participate in an employer-sponsored plan, his business cannot also have a plan eligible for the deduction.

Life Insurance

Other employee benefits that remain tax-free to the individual and tax-deductible to the corporation include life and disability insurance and workers' compensation insurance. "Free" life insurance purchased by the corporation for its employees is limited to one-year renewable term policies of up to $50,000 coverage per employee. Such insurance plans are normally set up for groups of employees, although even a sole owner-employee of a corporation can qualify under IRS guidelines.

The face value of the policy can exceed $50,000, but in such cases the IRS requires the individual to pay taxes on the "imputed income" above $50,000. Nor can the company take a tax deduction for the excess amount over $50,000. This taxable income is computed according to the age of the employee and the approximate amount of premium paid per $1,000. The following table from IRS publication 525 summarizes these variables:

Cost per $1,000 of Protection for One Month

Age*	Cost
Under 25	5 cents
25 through 29	6 cents
30 through 34	8 cents
35 through 39	9 cents
40 through 44	10 cents
45 through 49	15 cents
50 through 54	23 cents
55 through 59	43 cents
60 through 64	66 cents
65 through 69	$1.27
70 and older	$2.06

Age is determined at end of year (December 31).

You figure the cost for each month of coverage by multiplying the number of thousands of dollars of insurance, figured to the nearest tenth, by the cost from the above table. You must prorate the cost from the table if less than a full month of coverage is involved For example, you are 54 years old and your employer provides term life insurance coverage for you in the amount of $80,000. Since $50,000 is excludable from your income, you must figure the amount to include in your income of the remaining $30,000 in coverage. The cost per $1,000 of someone 54 years old is 23 cents (from table). Multiply this figure times 30 (the number of thousands of dollars of the excess amount). This figure of $6.90 (23 cents x 30) is the cost of excess insurance for one month. The amount for the year, $82.80 (12 x $6.90), is the figure that you would show on your personal income tax return as income.

You can also set up an insurance program that gives retired employees (including yourself) up to $50,000 per person of tax-deductible insurance. The retiree would be liable for taxes on insurance above $50,000. Furthermore, you can arrange for group life insurance for immediate family members of the corporation's employees.

Disability Insurance

Premiums paid by your corporation for disability insurance coverage are also deductible by the corporation and tax-free to the employee(s). Although the amount of disability insurance an employee can purchase is limited to a percentage of income, usually in the range of 33 to 60 percent,[9] for higher paid executives the premiums per year may amount to thousands of dollars in tax-free "income." Benefits paid under company-financed plans for temporary disability (illness or injury) are included in the employee's gross income and are subject to tax.[10] In the case of permanent and total disability, a partial tax exclusion of benefits is allowed. If the premiums for disability insurance are paid by the employee, however, all benefits, whether for temporary or permanent disability, are non-taxable.

Workers' Compensation

Workers' compensation is another form of insurance deductible by your corporation. Workers' compensation insurance set by state law covers any claims for bodily injuries or job-related diseases suffered by employees in your business regardless of fault. This form of insurance is not even available to sole proprietors, but you are entitled to it as the employee of your corporation.[11]

Interest-free and Low-interest Loans

Another benefit that key employees or sole owner-operators of corporations have enjoyed for decades is interest-free loans.

For interest-free or below market interest loans made or outstanding after June 6, 1984, the following rules apply. Such loans from the employer to the employee or independent contractor will be treated as though the employee or independent contractor received compensation equal to the market rate of interest that would have been due if the money had been borrowed from a conventional source such as a bank. This imputed compensation must be included in the gross income of the borrower; if the borrower itemizes deductions, he can take an offsetting deduction for the imputed interest expense, however. In order to get the interest deduction at present, the loan must be secured by your home. The interest will then be deductible as home equity loan interest, unless you already have the maximum $100,000 of home equity debt.

Such treatment would normally produce a "wash," without taxable income to the employee, unless the loan was used to carry tax-exempt securities (in which case, no interest deduction is permitted). This interest-free loan perk can be made available to executives of a corporation on a discriminatory basis, that is, it does not have to be offered to all employees or even ones of a particular class or group. Such loans can be made for

---

[9] Insurance companies limit benefits to avoid creating a disincentive to return to work. Why would they need to do that?

[10] The "sick pay exclusion" which in the past treated such benefits as tax-free income was repealed by the Tax Reform Act of 1976.

[11] A partnership, moreover, cannot deduct premiums paid for workers' compensation on behalf of partners, since partners are not considered employees of the partnership.

virtually any purpose, from buying a home to financing a child's education.

It is important to note that loans under $10,000 are not treated as though an imputed amount of interest were received and then paid back. In other words, a $10,000 *de minimis* exception allows loans of this size or smaller to be treated in the old conventional way as interest-free and tax-free.

Corporate-shareholder loans also are subject to the $10,000 *de minimis* exception. For loans in excess of $10,000 in this area, the imputed interest is treated as transferred from the corporation to the shareholder. Thus the corporation is considered to have paid a dividend includable in the shareholder's income. The shareholder gets an offsetting deduction, however, and the corporation treats as interest income the amount of imputed interest.
The current rate of imputed interest will be set semi-annually by the Treasury Department, based on market conditions. The law does not make clear whether those individuals who have dual roles as shareholders and employees in a corporation are to be treated under the employer-employee rule or the corporation-shareholder rule.

If you have a corporate pension plan, you can also borrow from it, but the rules prohibit no-interest, below market loans.

Regarding Illinois state law, the statutes authorize your corporation to make loans to you as an employee, officer, or director *for any purpose.* This has not always been the case. In the past, such loans were permitted only for the purpose of providing homes for employees. Now, the loan may be with or without interest, and may be secured or unsecured, as the board deems appropriate. Such loans offer one attractive way of taking money out of your business for legitimate personal uses. It is important to exercise the proper formality in recording all such loans, by signing a promissory note and carrying the loan on the company record books under "Accounts Receivable." By following a strict repayment schedule, you will avoid personal trouble with the IRS on the issue of whether the loan is actually a disguised dividend.

Tax-free Dividends
Dividends paid to you personally by *any* corporation are fully taxable as ordinary income. By contrast, if the same stock investments were made by your corporation, 70 percent of the total dividends would escape taxes. The limitations on what qualifies for tax-free treatment are spelled out in IRS Publication 542. Basically, all dividends from domestic U.S. stocks qualify for the 70 percent exclusion, except for dividends from a real estate investment trust and dividends from stock held by your corporation for 45 days or less (90 days or less for preferred dividends).

There exist mutual funds for corporations that invest in stocks that pay dividend income qualifying for the 70 percent corporate exclusion from tax. Two such funds are Vanguard

Qualified Dividend Portfolio 1 and Fidelity Qualified Dividend Fund.

Naturally, you will want to maximize your passive income earnings through dividends and other sources. One word of caution, however: you do not want to be considered a "personal holding corporation" by the IRS. A personal holding corporation is defined as a company in which 60 percent or more of corporate profits consists of passive income from stocks, bonds, rents, royalties, etc., and less than 40 percent of profits derives from business operations. If you do not limit your investment income and are deemed a personal holding company, you will be subject to especially heavy punitive taxes.

Other Tax-deductible Benefits and Expenses

The payment of rent, utility, and phone bills for business usage all provide legitimate tax deductions for your corporation. If your office is at home, then you will need to allocate your expenses between business and personal use. If you rent an apartment, it is a good idea to write two checks each month, one business and one personal, for the proportionate part of the total rent in each case. A proportionate percentage of other expenses such as water and electricity can also be deducted by your corporation.[12]

If you have a separate business phone, then the total bill will, of course, be a business expense. If one phone serves both business and personal use, you should keep a log of all long-distance business calls and be sure to pay the full amount of these as a corporate expense. Before 1989, you could deduct the part of the base rate of your residential telephone allocable to business usage. Currently, the base rate of the first telephone into your residence is considered a nondeductible personal living expense, with no business portion allowable.

If you own your home and have an office therein, you can rent office space to the corporation. Rent paid to a stockholder is another area the IRS looks at closely, since excessive rent provides one way for owners of a corporation to take disguised dividends out of the company. Therefore, the amount of rent you charge the corporation should be reasonable in terms of the cost of comparable office space in your vicinity. If you use 10 percent of your home as an office, do not figure the corporate rent as 10 percent of your mortgage and taxes, however. Generally, you will be entitled to a larger deduction than this when you consider what similar office space rents for. You should draw up a formal lease agreement with the corporation, in the event of a future tax audit.

You can also deduct "repairs" to the business portion of your property in the

---

[12] A higher percentage may be justified for the business portion in individual cases. Your

business may require unusually large expenditures for electricity and water if you are a professional photographer or a beautician, for example.

year incurred, while "improvements" must be amortized over the period of time they are expected to last.

Other tax-free employee benefits that may be provided include free parking, group legal service plans that offer up to $70 in legal services per employee annually (any amount over that would be taxable to the employee), subsidized lunches, and on-site physical fitness facilities.

In the case of parking, the employer can pay each employee's parking expenses up to the amount of $185 per month as a tax-free subsidy. The employer may also provide up to $100 a month per employee as a tax-free mass transit subsidy.

The reimbursement of expenses for operating and maintaining automobiles and other motor vehicles used in your business are deductible either on a per-mile or actual cost basis.

The depreciation of business equipment such as cars and computers is another form of tax-free benefit. An especially attractive tax break is the current law allowing up to $25,000 of business property to be written off in the first year that it is placed in service (instead of depreciated).[13] Special rules concerning this write-off apply to cars.

Your corporation can also pay and deduct up to $5,000 as a tax-free death benefit to the beneficiary of any employee, including yourself.

Eucational expenses up to $5,250 per employee are also deductible by the corporation and tax-free to the recipient.[14] Your company could pay for tuition, books, supplies, and other education-related equipment for either work-related or non-job-related courses taken by employees (but not for those graduate courses leading to a degree in law, business, medicine, or other advanced or professional degrees). The eligibility of such a program depends on

(1) its being in written form
(2) the giving of reasonable notice of the plan and its terms and availability to all eligible employees and
(3) its not being discriminatory in favor of certain officers, shareholders, or key employees, or spouses or dependents of such individuals.

There is also a stringent restriction on the amount of benefits available to shareholders of the corporation: no more than 5 percent of the benefits paid or incurred by the employer during the year can go to that group of individuals (and their dependents) each of whom holds more than a 5 percent interest in the company.

Other tax-free benefits include the cost of convention travel as well as food, lodging, and related expenses incurred by employees attending meetings to increase business know-how and to upgrade skills. Foreign conventions, with several exceptions, are generally *not* deductible, although travel abroad for business purposes *is* deductible.

---

[13] This write-off amount is scheduled to be raised to a $25,000 annual deduction in the year 2003 and beyond.

[14] This perk has now been made permanent by Congress, after years of annual renewals.

Your corporation can also give you and other employees a discount on goods and services. The Tax Reform Act of 1984 placed a limit on the amount of such tax-free discounts. The discount is now limited to your "gross profit percentage." If your profit margin averages 30 percent, then any discount over this percentage will be taxable. The discount must be available to all employees on a non-discriminatory basis. You can also offer up to a 20 percent tax-free discount on services.

Finally, a corporation, unlike a sole proprietorship or a partnership, can deduct charitable contributions up to 10 percent of its taxable income. Contributions in excess of this limitation can be carried over and deducted for up to five succeeding years, subject to certain limitations. Your corporation thus gives you the opportunity, unavailable to the sole proprietor or partnership, to support a favorite charity or cause with tax-deductible business dollars.

Chapter 5. Forming Your Own Illinois Corporation

If you have carefully read the preceding chapters and have decided that you are one of the many individuals who can benefit from the corporate form of business, you are now ready to learn about the procedure for setting up your own for-profit Illinois corporation.[1]

Corporate Name

The first step in organizing your profit corporation is the choice of a name for your business that you like and that complies with state law. The Illinois statutes specify that your corporate name must contain either the word "corporation," "incorporated," "company," "limited," or an abbreviation of one of these words ("corp.," "inc.," "co.," or "ltd."). Also, the name you select must be *distinguishable* from the following:

(1) names of other profit corporations (domestic or foreign) authorized to do business in Illinois

(2) names of not for profit Illinois corporations.

If you are presently running a business in the state as a sole proprietor or partner, you can use the same business name for your corporation as you currently have by just adding "Inc.," provided that another business in one of the above categories is not now operating in Illinois under the same name. Even if the name you choose for your corporation is your own name, you still will not be able to use it if it turns out that someone is already doing business in Illinois under that exact name, unless you modify it in some way to clearly distinguish your business name from the other person's.

Just because your name happens to be Walgreen, don't imagine that you can open another Walgreen's Drug Store in Libertyville. But perhaps a Walgreen Dry Cleaners will work, provided one is not already registered with the Illinois Secretary of State.

---

[1] If you are considering forming a professional service corporation as a doctor, dentist, engineer, etc., we suggest that you read this chapter first, then Chapter 6, which deals specifically with the Illinois professional service corporation. Also see Chapter 7, regarding the Illinois not for profit corporation.

The Name's The Thing

The P. Gaines Co. publishes a helpful and widely reviewed book on selecting names for use in commerce, **Naming Your Business and Its Products and Services: How to Create Effective Trade Names, Trademarks, and Service Marks to Attract Customers, Protect Your Good Will and Reputation, and Stay Out of Court!** *Every business, whether a corporation, a partnership, a sole proprietorship, or a limited liability company needs to have a business name under which it conducts its affairs. Need we point out that it is important that such a name be legal, from the standpoint of trademark law, as well as catchy? This guide will show you how to have the best of both worlds. See the order form in the back of this book.*

In the event that you do incorporate, it is important to realize that even though the business name you select for your company is approved by the Illinois Secretary of State, this is no guarantee of the legality of the use of the name from the standpoint of trademark law. You may still be sued by an incorporated or unincorporated company in Illinois or in another state if the name chosen is the same as or deceptively similar to that of the other company's.

The use of your family surname (Smith's Pet Care) as your business name, furthermore, is often the worst possible choice, for several reasons. *Naming Your Business and Its Products*

and Services fully explains these and other significant issues in the business name selection process, whether that of a trade name, trademark, or service mark.

In addition, your company name cannot falsely imply professional affiliation or mislead in other ways. "Architect," "Landscape Architect," "Engineer," "Surveyor," and derivative terms may only be used by professional service corporations that have complied with the requirements of the state board of registration of that profession as well as all applicable statutory provisions. Your company name cannot falsely imply government affiliation nor suggest the conduct of business as a bank or a savings and loan or an insurance company.

The name of the corporation need not be in the English language, provided that it is written in English letters or Arabic or Roman numerals.

Since you have to include the name of your corporation in the Articles of Incorporation that you file with the Secretary of State, you may want to reserve the name you have decided on in advance. You can submit a written application requesting the use of a specified name as the name of your corporation (along with a twenty five-dollar filing fee). A copy of the form (BCA-4.10) that you may use to reserve a corporate name is included in the back of this book in Appendix E. If the name specified in your application is available, you will be given the exclusive right to use it as the name of your corporation for 90 days.

If you are in a hurry to incorporate, the quickest procedure is to ask for a telephone confirmation of the availability of a particular name by calling 1-217-782-9520. Someone will check immediately while you wait to see if the name you want is available. You can also check name availability on the business services website: *www.cyberdrive illinois.com.* Click on the "Services for Business" icon, and then select "Corporation Search." Type your proposed name in the box for an instant search of existing names. Although a telephone check or web search is a reliable indication in most cases, it does not absolutely guarantee the availability of a particular name that is cleared in this fashion. The Secretary of State reserves the right to make its final decision on the matter when a name reservation request has been approved or Articles of Incorporation have been filed.

As a necessary precaution, do not have business stationery or customized stock certificates printed or make other commitments to a name until the Articles have been filed, approved, and returned to you.

To save time, it may be a good idea to either reserve your name in advance or at least have a preliminary name check via phone. Otherwise, your Articles will be returned to you unfiled if the name you have chosen has already been taken, and you will have to refile again under another name. . . and again. . .and again, until you hit on a name that isn't currently being used. A little foresight

and advance planning will eliminate these potential delays.

The Articles of Incorporation

In order to obtain corporate status, you will now need to fill out and mail to the Secretary of State two copies of your Articles of Incorporation (Form BCA-2.10). This form is simple to complete in most cases. A copy of this form is available in Appendix A in the back of this book. If the form has already been removed or you have a library edition of this book whose forms are not of the tear-out variety, additional copies can be obtained by writing the Illinois Secretary of State, Corporation Department, The Howlett Building, Third Floor, Springfield, Illinois 62756, Telephone (217) 782-6961.

Forms may also be requested in the Chicago area by mail or phone from Office of the Secretary of State, The Corporation Department, 17 W. State Street, Suite 1137, Chicago, Illinois 60602, Telephone (312) 793-3380. When completing the form, which must be filled out in the English language, you should either type or print clearly in black ink all information.

The following two pages present you with a sample Articles of Incorporation. **Article 1**, the name of the corporation, we have already discussed. Be sure to consult our publication, *Naming Your Business and Its Products and Services,*

Form **BCA-2.10** | ARTICLES OF INCORPORATION

(Rev. Jan. 1999)

Jesse White
Secretary of State
Department of Business Services
Springfield, IL 62756
http://www.sos.state.il.us

Payment must be made by certified check, cashier's check, Illinois attorney's check, Illinois C.P.A's check or money order, payable to "Secretary of State."

This space for use by Secretary of State

SUBMIT IN DUPLICATE!

This space for use by Secretary of State

Date

Franchise Tax $
Filing Fee $

Approved:

1. CORPORATE NAME: _____ WANDA GOLD ENTERPRISES, INC. _____

(The corporate name must contain the word "corporation", "company," "incorporated," "limited" or an abbreviation thereof.)

2. Initial Registered Agent: Wanda   X.   Gold

First Name	Middle Initial	Last name

Initial Registered Office: 1829 Moose Avenue

Number	Street	Suite #
Chicago IL	Cook	60612
City	County	Zip Code

3. Purpose or purposes for which the corporation is organized:
(If not sufficient space to cover this point, add one or more sheets of this size.)

THE TRANSACTION OF ANY OR ALL LAWFUL BUSINESSES FOR WHICH
CORPORATIONS MAY BE INCORPORATED UNDER THE BUSINESS
CORPORATION ACT OF 1983.

4. Paragraph 1: Authorized Shares, Issued Shares and Consideration Received:

Class	Par Value per Share	Number of Shares Authorized	Number of Shares Proposed to be Issued	Consideration to be Received Therefor
Common	$ No par value	3,000	400	$ 16,000.00

TOTAL = $ 16,000.00

Paragraph 2: The preferences, qualifications, limitations, restrictions and special or relative rights in respect of the shares of each class are:
(If not sufficient space to cover this point, add one or more sheets of this size.)

5. *OPTIONAL:*   (a) Number of directors constituting the initial board of directors of the corporation: _____3_____ .
   (b) Names and addresses of the persons who are to serve as directors until the first annual meeting of shareholders or until their successors are elected and qualify:

Name	Residential Address	City, State, ZIP
Wanda Gold	1829 Moose Avenue	Chicago, IL 60612
Junior Gold	912 Virtue Blvd	Chicago, IL 60637
Giesela Gold	814 Persimmon Lane	Chicago, IL 60301

6. *OPTIONAL:*   (a) It is estimated that the value of all property to be owned by the corporation for the following year wherever located will be: $ _____
   (b) It is estimated that the value of the property to be located within the State of Illinois during the following year will be: $ _____
   (c) It is estimated that the gross amount of business that will be transacted by the corporation during the following year will be: $ _____
   (d) It is estimated that the gross amount of business that will be transacted from places of business in the State of Illinois during the following year will be: $ _____

7. *OPTIONAL:*   OTHER PROVISIONS
   Attach a separate sheet of this size for any other provision to be included in the Articles of Incorporation, e.g., authorizing preemptive rights, denying cumulative voting, regulating internal affairs, voting majority requirements, fixing a duration other than perpetual, etc.

8. ## NAME(S) & ADDRESS(ES) OF INCORPORATOR(S)

The undersigned incorporator(s) hereby declare(s), under penalties of perjury, that the statements made in the foregoing Articles of Incorporation are true.

Dated _____January 4_____ , _2003_
      (Month & Day)   Year

Signature and Name   **Address**

1. _Wanda Gold (signature)_   1. _1829 Moose Avenue_
   Signature   Street
   Wanda Gold   _Chicago, Illinois 60612_
   (Type or Print Name)   City/Town   State   ZIP Code

2. _____   2. _____
   Signature   Street

   _____   _____
   (Type or Print Name)   City/Town   State   ZIP Code

3. _____   3. _____
   Signature   Street

   _____   _____
   (Type or Print Name)   City/Town   State   ZIP Code

(Signatures must be in **BLACK INK** on original document. Carbon copy, photocopy or rubber stamp signatures may only be used on conformed copies.)
NOTE: If a corporation acts as incorporator, the name of the corporation and the state of incorporation shall be shown and the execution shall be by its president or vice president and verified by him, and attested by its secretary or assistant secretary.

FEE SCHEDULE

- The initial franchise tax is assessed at the rate of 15/100 of 1 percent ($1.50 per $1,000) on the paid-in capital represented in this state, with a minimum of $25.
- The filing fee is $75.
- The **minimum total due** (franchise tax + filing fee) is **$100.**
  (Applies when the Consideration to be Received as set forth in Item 4 does not exceed $16,667)
- The Department of Business Services in Springfield will provide assistance in calculating the total fees if necessary.

Illinois Secretary of State   Springfield, IL 62756
Department of Business Services   Telephone (217) 782-9522 or 782-9523   C-162.20

before making your final name selection, to alert you to the legal pitfalls of a poorly chosen moniker and the potential rewards of an effective and legally defensible commercial name (see the listing in the back of this book for details on this publication). Assuming you have found an available name to your liking, you can fill it in here.

Article 2 asks for information about the registered office and the registered agent of the corporation. The purpose of this information is to provide for public record a legal mailing address and contract person to receive corporate mailings from the Secretary of State, as well as legal documents (summons, subpoenas) in connection with any lawsuits that might arise against the corporation. The registered agent must be a resident of Illinois and would ordinarily be one of the corporate directors. The registered office must be located in Illinois, and its street address given (post office box alone not acceptable). In theory, you could authorize anyone residing in Illinois to act as your registered agent, such an attorney or friend.[2] If you are the sole owner-operator of the proposed corporation, you can simply fill in your own name as the registered agent and your business address as the address of the registered office. Any changes in the address of the registered office or the name of the registered agent at a later date must, of course, be filed with the

Secretary of State. Failure to file such information may result in the dissolution of the corporation's Articles.

Article 3 pertains to the purpose of the corporation. This article should be filled in as follows:

THE TRANSACTION OF ANY OR ALL LAWFUL BUSINESSES FOR WHICH CORPORATIONS MAY BE INCORPORATED UNDER THE BUSINESS CORPORATION ACT OF 1983.

It is important to note that a general purpose clause such as this may *not* be used for not for profit corporations (see Chapter 7) and professional service corporations (see Chapter 6). In most other cases, it is no longer necessary or even advisable to enumerate the specific types of business activities you are incorporating. By making this clause as broad as possible, you allow the future possibility of entering into related or even totally unrelated business activities, without the necessity of having to organize another corporation for that specific purpose or to amend the Articles of Incorporation of your existing business. Although today you are operating a shoe store, tomorrow you may meet someone in the scuba diving business and decide to pursue a whole new line. There are legal advantages to general purpose clauses as well, as in the case of an *ultra vires* lawsuit brought by a dissenting shareholder.[3]

---

[2] There exist corporations that provide registered offices and registered agents for other corporations, but these companies are normally used as agents by large corporations with offices in a number of states or "foreign" corporations doing business in Illinois.

---

[3] An *ultra vires* act is one in which a corporate officer or director has exceeded his authority as granted by the Articles of Incorporation or corporate bylaws.

Article 4 concerns the issue of stock. According to our recommendations in Chapter 2, you would authorize stock of common class, no-par value, with a large number of authorized shares (3,000, for instance). We have suggested that the number of shares actually *issued* be much smaller than the number authorized. Thus, if you authorized 3,000 shares in Article 4, a smaller number of issued shares would usually be appropriate (300, for example). In this way, you can later issue additional shares if need be. In the future, you may wish to issue additional shares in order to add more capital to your business. As long as you do not issue more than the original number authorized in your Articles of Incorporation, you will not need to report these transactions to the state and pay a fee.

The "consideration to be received therefor" is the amount of capital you and other stockholders will pay in exchange for shares of stock. Any amount of capital in cash, property, accounts receivable, inventories, etc. may be initially put into your business when you incorporate, or none. We do recommend beginning with enough start-up capital in your corporation to take care of foreseeable short-term expenses.

You don't want to overcapitalize your corporation, on the other hand, since you will more quickly reach the ceiling set by the IRS for accumulated earnings. At that point, money paid to stockholders will usually take the form of dividends, subject to the "double tax" discussed previously. This is generally not a concern for firms with $100,000 or less in start-up capital.

An aside: one good way to keep from tying up more capital than necessary when you incorporate is to provide part of the initial seed money in the form of a short-term loan to the corporation. The corporation need not pay you interest on the loan as long as it is truly of short-term duration, say, three months or less and is not more than about $5,000. If it turns out that the corporation needs this loan money for an extended period of time to stay afloat, however, you may run into problems with the IRS in later taking the money out of the corporation.[4] To avoid running afoul of the ever-watchful authorities, larger start-up loans for longer periods of time should carry an interest charge at market rates, which is a deductible expense for the corporation.

Paragraph 2 of Article 4 allows space to indicate any preferences, qualifications, limitations, or restrictions on the shares of stock to be authorized and issued. This paragraph will not apply to many small corporations. You can simply leave the space blank, unless you plan to issue more than one class of stock. If you will have two or more classes of stock, Paragraph 2 must be completed. If you will have two or more classes of common stock, the differences that distinguish these classes must be

---

[4] The IRS may argue that this money is not actually a loan at all but equity capital needed for day-to-day operations. Therefore, the return of this money would be considered for tax purposes as a dividend and would be taxable to the recipient.

described. Classes may vary with respect to voting rights, management terms, transferability rights, or preemptive rights.

Most small corporations, as noted, will not need to have different classes of common stock. There is one case where even certain small corporations may at some point find it advantageous to issue two classes of stock, however. Some small corporations may wish to issue two classes of common stock, one voting and the other nonvoting, in the case of some family corporations that want to keep control of the corporation within the hands of several (or even one) family members, while giving other family members shares of dividend-paying stock.

If you decide to have different classes of stock, the rights of each class concerning voting privileges, dividends, and so on will have to be decided and indicated in Article Four. Since there are a number of different rights, preferences, and limitations assignable to stock, legal consultation is advisable if you wish to have two or more classes of stock. Also, you should check with the Illinois Division of Securities if you propose to authorize more than one class of stock, to be sure the wording of your stock provisions meets their approval.

Regarding the question of "common" vs. "preferred" stock, as noted previously, preferred stock is so named because shareholders of this type of stock receive their dividends first, before all other classes of stock, at a fixed rate of return. Common stock is paid after preferred, at a variable rate depending on the current profitability of the corporation. If the corporation is dissolved, preferred stockholders also would receive preferential treatment in the division of the corporate assets. The right to receive dividends before any dividends are paid out to the holders of the common shares is the most usual preference that preferred shares enjoy. The Illinois Business Corporation Act mentions others rights and terms that qualify as "preferred" provisions as well, such as: whether shares of any class shall be convertible into shares of any other class and the rate of such conversion right; whether the corporation itself shall have the right to redeem shares at a price not exceeding that fixed in the Articles of Incorporation; whether the rights to dividends are cumulative, partially cumulative, or noncumulative; whether and to what extent any class shall have preference as to asets upon liquidation.

If you don't understand these terms, don't worry. You don't need to be able to manipulate these terms in order to form a corporation, since they are terms that will make sense only to those initiated into the mysteries of classes of stock through active involvement in stock investing. Many publicly traded corporations listed on the New York and American Stock Exchanges have both preferred and common stock, but small, privately held corporations usually have no need to issue preferred stock.

Three optional articles, **Article 5, Article 6, and Article 7**, are also included on the form. These pertain, respectively, to:

(1) the determination of the number of directors that the corporation will have initially and the designation of their names and addresses.

One advantage of naming the first board of directors in the Articles is that you will not have to call the organizational meeting of the incorporators for this purpose. As soon as the Articles are filed by the Illinois Department of Business Services, the board may get on with the business of the corporation.

(2) estimates of the worth of the corporation in the first year of business.

Only corporations that are doing business in other states in addition to Illinois need fill in Article 6. If it is left blank, you are acknowledging in essence that all your property and business are located in Illinois and that 100 percent of your paid-in capital, as indicated in your Articles, is taxable in Illinois.

(3) other provisions.

If you wish to add any other provisions, attach a separate sheet of paper of any size with the provision(s) and head it with the next article number following the last one filled out on the printed form. For example, if the last article you completed on the printed form was Article 5, then head your attachment "Article 6."

Article 7 on the printed form allows the incorporator(s) to specify various additional points, if desired, such as fixing a duration of the corporation other than perpetual, denying cumulative voting rights, choosing to run the corporation according to a shareholder's agreement under the Close Corporation Act. Since the "life" of a corporation is assumed to be perpetual in Illinois unless stated otherwise, you may specify a fixed period for your corporation on this added page or pages. Such a fixed-life corporation might be appropriate in the case of a corporation organized for the purposes of conducting a political campaign, for instance. If you wish to deny your corporation the right to have cumulative voting (explained in Chapter 2, pages 31-32), this should be specified here also.

Another major area often covered by additional points is that pertaining to a close corporation agreement. Illinois law does make a distinction between this type of corporation and a regular corporation. The main purpose of the close corporation option is to allow the shareholder(s) of a corporation a way to regulate any aspect of the internal affairs of the corporation or the relations of the shareholders among themselves. The running of the corporation under a so-called "shareholders' agreement" (without a board of directors and other formalities) is permitted and may be specified here. The placing of restrictions upon the transfer of stock to outsiders is also allowed.

See Appendix E for a list of the various options available under a close corporation agreement and the slightly different manner in which the Articles of Incorporation form is to be filled out. Designed for small or even one-man or one-woman corporations, the close corporation is a sensible option for many. In one-person corporations, the elimination of the board of directors is frequently a necessity, for instance.

It is a good idea to maintain a minimum of formality by having traditional offices, that of a president and secretary-treasurer at least, even if the same person holds both offices. Those completely informal corporations that dispense with both corporate officers and directors by means of a shareholders agreement may encounter difficulties in getting bank loans, dealing with the IRS, and so on

Article 8 requests the date of incorporation, the name(s) and address(es) of the incorporator(s), and his/her (their) signature(s). Either a residence or a business address may be provided, consisting of a street number and name, city, and state.

The two completed copies of the Articles of Incorporation (two originals or one original and one photocopy) are filed with the Secretary of State's Corporation Division, Mail to the address on the back of the form, along with the appropriate fee:

Illinois for-profit corporations pay a minimum fee of $100.

Determine the amount of money you will pay to incorporate in the following manner. Two fees are involved, a franchise tax, and a filing fee. We have already discussed the franchise tax in Chapter 4. As noted, the initial frnachise tax is figured as 15/100 of 1 percent of paid-in capital.[5] That is, $1.50 per $1,000 of capital with a minimum tax of $25 will be due. All corporations with starting assets worth $16,667 or less will pay the same franchise tax of $25. Corporations with assets greater than $16,667 will, of course, pay a larger initial franchise tax. A corporation with $60,000 in assets will owe an initial franchise tax of $90, for instance.

The filing fee is set at $75 for all corporations.

The following summarizes these two fees:

• Corporate franchise tax: $1.50 per $1,000 of paid-in capital (minimum tax of $25).
• Filing fee of $75
• Minimum corporation: $100 in total fees

In order to verify the correct total fee owed in your case or to have someone compute it for you, you may phone the Corporation Department in Chicago, Telephone (312) 793-3380, or in Springfield, Telephone (217) 782-6961. Payment must be made in the exact amount due and in the form of a money order, cashier's check, certified check, an Illinois attorney's check, or an Illinois CPA's check. Personal checks and cash are not acceptable.

---

[5] The amount of the franchise tax is based upon a fixed percentage of "the total consideration to be received" by the corporation for its issued shares of stock.

Expedited Service for Filing of Incorporation Papers

Illinois has jointed a number of other states in offering expedited service for those requiring "rush" treatment of their corporate filings. While normal processing requires five to seven working days, expedited service is rendered in a 24-hour period. Also, if you walk the papers to the Secretary of State's office in Springfield (Room 350 of the Howlett Building), they will do the incorporation while you wait, usually a ten to twenty-minute procedure. An additional fee of $50 is charged for expedited filing of the Articles of Incorporation. Beginning in 2002, the Chicago office will also offer expedited service at 69 W. Washington Street, Suite 1240. Phone (312) 743-3380 for further details.

Recording the Articles of Incorporation

After the Articles of Incorporation have been correctly filed with the Secretary of State, one copy will be mailed back to you, attached to a Certificate of Incorporation (suitable for framing!). This entire document must be filed for record as soon as possible with the Office of the Recorder of Deeds (the specific county will depend on the location of the corporation's principal office). If your main or only corporate office is situated in Cook County, for instance, the Recorder and Registrar of Titles at 118 N. Clark, Chicago, Illinois 60602, Telephone (312) 443-5050, will handle your recording.

This office charges $23.50 for recording the first two printed sides plus $2.00 for each additional side. The cost of recording a single-sheet Articles of Incorporation (with two sides of printing) and a Certificate (printed on one side), will therefore amount to $25.50. You may go to the office and have these papers recorded in person, or you can mail them in. In either case, money orders and any checks but personal ones are acceptable. If you mail your papers to the Recorder, be sure to enclose a stamped, self-addressed envelope for their return. Specific instructions for recording Articles of Incorporation in other counties are available through the office of the Recorder of Deeds and Titles for the county of your chief corporate office. When these documents have been properly recorded, they will be returned to you. Thereafter they must be kept as part of the permanent records of the corporation.

Transferring Assets and Liabilities to Your New Corporation

When you are ready to start business as a corporation, if you are beginning from scratch, you will simply turn over the assets that you are offering to the corporation as start-up capital in exchange for stock. The actual transfer procedure will be discussed below under "Issuing Shares of Stock."

If you already have a going business (sole proprietorship or partnership), the transfer will be a bit more complicated, since you have the option of transferring liabilities as well as assets. Legal counsel is advisable to assure the best arrangement tax-wise in your individual circumstances. Generally speaking, the total amount of liabilities transferred (accounts payable is one type of liability, for example) should not exceed the total amount of assets transferred (accounts receivable, inventories, etc.). Since the individual is personally relieved of his liabilities when he forms a corporation and transfers the debts to it, the amount of the net debt assumed by the company is considered a taxable benefit. The IRS will thus regard the excess of liabilities over assets as a cash payment that is taxable to the individual.

To be on the safe side, you can always balance your assets and liabilities by donating some personal assets to the corporation, such as a typewriter, a computer, a file cabinet, a desk, and so on. Of course, if the assets transferred are greater than the liabilities, there is no problem—only the reverse imbalance will result in punitive taxes.

If you transfer the entire business to the corporation, including inventory, capital assets, accounts payable and receivable, the IRS will not tax the uncollected receivables as long as you meet one test. You have to receive control of at least 80 percent of the new corporation (including a minimum of 80 percent of voting stock as well as 80 percent of non-voting stock, if applicable).

In Chapter 1, the possibility of taking back only a portion of the value of your appraised business in stock was mentioned. By receiving only $40,000 in stock in partial payment for a business worth, say, $200,000, the balance of $160,000 is treated as a loan from you to the corporation. The corporation consequently issues you a note for $160,000 and pays you back this sum, plus interest, over the term of years you specify in the note. Such an arrangement has the decided advantage of producing mostly tax-free income to you—only the *interest portion* will be taxable. The rest will be treated by the IRS as a return of principal, which is nontaxable.

You also have the option of shutting down your sole proprietorship or partnership, so that you commence business as a corporation on a fresh basis. It may take several months or more to wind down your old business. But you need not wait until this process is totally completed before starting your corporation. Just be sure to keep business records of the proprietorship or partnership separate from those of the corporation, for both tax and legal purposes. You will also want to notify creditors and clients in writing of the dissolution of the prior business and of the existence of the new corporation. This can be accomplished with a form letter accompanying your regular business mailings.

Ordering Corporate Records Book, Seal, and Stock Certificates

The Illinois Business Corporation Act requires that every Illinois corporation keep minutes of the meetings of its shareholders and board of directors, as well as a record of shareholders, giving the names and addresses of all shareholders, the number, classes, and series of shares held by each, and the dates when they became shareholders of record.

Illinois law does not require you to have a corporate seal, but many corporations do use one. You may be asked for the seal imprint on formal agreements such as the application for the corporate bank accounts, bank loan papers, and lease agreements. A seal can be ordered from most stationery stores at a cost of approximately $20 to $25 dollars. The corporate outfit advertised in the back of this book also contains a corporate seal. The corporate seal is circular and contains the name of the corporation exactly as filed with the Secretary of State, the name of the state (Illinois), the words "Corporate SEAL," and the year of incorporation.

Records

The P. Gaines Co. offers a reasonably priced and attractive complete corporate outfit, which includes a custom engraved seal, 20 custom printed stock certificates, 50 blank sheets of rag content 20-lb. bond Minute Paper as well as a binder for minutes, corporate bylaws, and stock records. Please refer to the back of this book for additional information about this individually customized corporate outfit and an order form.

While the Illinois statutes no longer require that certificates signed by officials of the corporation must represent shares of stock of Illinois profit corporations, we do recommend their use for small corporations as an effective means of organizing the corporation. The certificate is simply a concrete representation of one's capital holdings in a corporation. A certificate may be used to represent more than one share of stock. Each certificate shall state:

(1) That the corporation is organized under the laws of the state of Illinois.
(2) The name of the person to whom issued.
(3) The number of shares represented by the certificate.
(4) If the shares of the corporation are classified, the designation of the class of shares, and the designation of the series, if any, which such certificate represents.
(5) If the corporation is authorized to issue more than one class or series of shares, the designation, relative rights, preferences and limitations of the shares of each class or series of shares authorized to be issued, which shall be set forth on the front or back of the certificate, or a statement to the effect that the corporation will furnish to a shareholder all such information upon request.
(6) If the corporation is organized as a close corporation, as provided in the Illinois Close Corporation Act of 1977 (see Appendix E), every certificate representing shares issued by such corporation shall conspicuously set forth upon the face or back of the certificate a full statement of all

the restrictions on transfer and the qualifications of shareholders set forth in subparagraphs (a) and (b) of Section 3 of the Close Corporation Act and the existence of a written agreement regarding the conduct of the affairs of the corporation, as provided in Section 11 of the Act. Such full statement may be omitted from the certificate if it shall be conspicuously set forth upon the face or back of the certificate that such statement and written agreement, if any, in full, will be furnished by the corporation to any shareholder upon request and without charge.

It is standard procedure for corporations to imprint their stock certificates with their corporate seal. Stock certificates may be purchased from some larger stationery stores. The complete corporate outfit which the P. Gaines Co. offers contains 25 attractive certificates, custom printed with the corporate name, state, and officers' titles.

Preorganization Subscription Agreement

If you are a one-man band, then a subscription agreement will not be necessary. If other shareholders will be involved in setting up the corporation, however, you may wish to have them sign a "preorganization subscription agreement." This agreement is legally binding in the state of Illinois, provided that it is in writing and signed by the subscriber.

Once Articles of Incorporation are filed with the Secretary of State, all subscribers for shares shall be deemed to be shareholders of the corporation. The board of directors determines when subscriptions for shares are to be paid (normally immediately following the first board of directors meeting). The call for payment must be uniform for all the shareholders of the same class.

In the case of default, the corporation may proceed to collect the amount due in the same manner as any debt owed to the corporation. It may also rescind the subscription, sell the shares to a third party, and sue the defaulter for breach of contract. A sample subscription agreement follows on the next page. See Appendix E for a copy of this agreement that you can adopt for your own corporation. If you have more subscribers than can fit on one sheet, you can make as many additional copies of this form as necessary.

Preparing the Bylaws

You are now ready to prepare the bylaws for your corporation, which may contain any provision for the regulation or management of the affairs of the corporation that are not inconsistent with law or the Articles of Incorporation. The initial bylaws of an Illinois corporation shall be adopted by its shareholders or its board. The shareholders or the board may amend or repeal the bylaws or adopt new bylaws, unless power to do so is reserved exclusively to the shareholders by the

PREORGANIZATION SUBSCRIPTION AGREEMENT

We, the undersigned, severally subscribe to the number of shares set opposite our respective names of capital stock of a proposed corporation, to be known as

Wanda Gold Enterprises, Inc. _____ or by any other name that the members may select, and to be incorporated in the State of Illinois. We agree to pay the sum of $ __40__ per each share subscribed.

This subscription shall not be binding on the undersigned unless subscriptions in the aggregate amount of $ __$16,000.00__ for shares of said corporation have been procured on or before the __4th__ day of __January__ , 20 __03__.

All subscriptions hereto shall be payable at such time or times as the board of directors of said corporation may determine and shall be paid in cash, except as hereinafter indicated. (If any of the subscriptions are to be paid by transferring property or offering services to the corporation, a description of the property and/or services shall be attached hereto.)

Date	Name and Address	Number of Shares	Amount Subscribed
1-3-2003	Wanda Gold 1829 Moose Ave. Chicago, Illinois 60612	200	$8,000.00
1-3-03	Junior Gold 911 Virtue Blvd Chicago, IL 60637	100	4,000
1-4-03	Gisela Gold 814 Persimmon Lane Oak Park, Illinois 60301	100	$4,000.00

67

Articles of Incorporation. The shareholders may prescribe in the bylaws that any bylaw made by them shall not be altered or repealed by the board.

We provide in Appendix B in the back of this book a set of bylaws that you can modify for your corporation's use by filling in the blanks and making minor alterations. If you are having an attorney prepare your incorporation, be sure to ask if he is using a "kit" with standard regulations. If not, find out why, because you will pay dearly if he or she has to draw up customized bylaws (in most cases, not necessary).

First, indicate the name of your corporation at the top of the page. In Article I, write in the name of the city/village/township (cross out the ones that don't apply) and the county where the principal executive office of the corporation is located.

In Article II, Section 2, indicate the date and time (5th of May at 6 p.m., for example) on which the annual shareholders' meeting is to be held. This will be the same date as the regular directors' meeting (Article III, Section 5). Often this date is set shortly before or after the close of the corporation's fiscal year, so that both the previous year and the coming year's business can be discussed.

If you want your fiscal year to coincide with the calendar year, however (beginning on January 1 and ending on December 31), you will want to hold your annual meeting close to the date on which your corporation is initially organized. In Article III, Section 2, indicate the number of directors of the corporation. Read through the bylaws to familiarize yourself with the contents. We will assume that the bylaws will be approved at the first shareholders' meeting, although, as noted above, they may be approved by the directors as well.

First Meeting of Shareholders

After the corporation has been organized and the Articles of Incorporation filed with the Secretary of State and returned to you approved, the first meeting of shareholders can be convened.[6] It is advisable to have each shareholder sign a waiver of notice form (included in Appendix C), in order to skip formal notice requirements. If there is more than one shareholder, a chairman who will preside at the meeting and a secretary who will keep minutes should be appointed. Minutes of this meeting which may be adopted for most corporations are found in Appendix C.

The meeting should be advised that the Articles of Incorporation have been filed and approved. A resolution to approve the Articles and to accept their filing should be made. If a subscription

---

[6] As already pointed out, the Illinois Close Corporation Act of 1977 provides for the option of a shareholder's agreement whereby the corporate directors may be dispensed with and the business of the corporation conducted entirely by the shareholders.

agreement has been used, it should be read and formally approved also.

The chairman informs the shareholders of the number of directors to be elected (if applicable). Nominations are accepted and voted on. The Illinois statutes, as mentioned above, provide for the option of cumulative voting unless the Articles of Incorporation specifically deny them. As explained in Chapter 2, under cumulative voting procedures the number of votes each shareholder is entitled to is determined by multiplying the number of shares he or she holds by the number of directors to be elected.

In the case of the three-shareholder corporation of Wanda, Junior, and Giesela Gold, Wanda would have 300 votes and Junior and Giesela 150 votes each, if Wanda holds 100 shares and the other two have 50 shares each and three directors are to be elected. Each may cast all of his votes for one nominee or divide them among several candidates in any proportion desired. The purpose of cumulative voting is to give minority shareholders greater voting power and representation than would otherwise be the case with statutory voting.

After the election of directors, the corporate bylaws are presented for approval. A majority of the voting power represented by the shareholders will constitute approval. After the meeting of shareholders is adjourned, the directors hold their first meeting (assuming that your corporation will have directors).

First Meeting of the Board of Directors

The purpose of the first meeting of the board is to elect officers, adopt the corporate seal and stock certificates, establish a fiscal year, decide on a bank or banks where the corporation will maintain accounts, and to make other types of resolutions. In Appendix D in the back of this book, you will find a set of corporate minutes that may be adopted for the first meeting of the board of directors. You will fill in the blanks with the pertinent information for your corporation and neatly cross out any resolutions that are not applicable to you.

We will go step by step through the first meeting and the preparation of the minutes. First, tear out the "Waiver of Notice," which is the first form in Appendix D, and fill in the blanks, indicating the date, time, and place of the meeting and have all the directors sign it.

One of the directors is to be chosen chairman and to preside, while another director should be selected to act as secretary. The secretary will complete the first page of the minutes by filling in the time, place, and date of the meeting and the names of the directors present as well as any absentees. The names of the acting chairman and the secretary are to be shown in the spaces provided.

The meeting should be advised of the filing of the Articles of Incorporation and their approval by the Secretary of State. The filing date should be recorded in the appropriate place in the minutes. The meeting thereafter acknowledges the adoption of the bylaws by the shareholders.

An election of officers should be conducted. When completed, the permanent secretary and president will replace the temporary ones appointed previously. The names of the officers elect are shown in the spaces provided in the minutes. As discussed in Chapter 2 under "Officers," one person may hold more than one or even all the offices, if the Articles or the bylaws so provide.

When the resolution concerning the corporate seal has been read and passed, the secretary should make an impression of the seal in the space provided in the right-hand margin. A resolution to adopt the type of stock certificate to be issued by the corporation follows next.

The location of the principal executive office of the corporation should next be entered in the spaces provided.

The directors must establish a fiscal year for the corporation. It is simplest to have your fiscal year coincide with the calendar year (beginning January 1 and ending December 31). You also have the option of having your fiscal year be another twelve-month period ending on the last day of a month other than December (May 1 to April 30, for example). Another possibility allowed by the IRS is to have your fiscal year end on the same day of the week in the same month each year, for instance, the last Friday in June. In this case, your fiscal year will have 52 weeks during

some years and 53 weeks in other years. Since various tax and accounting questions are connected to the establishment of a fiscal year, you may want to consult a tax adviser about this issue. Fill in the information concerning the fiscal year in the minutes.

The choice of a bank or banks for corporate accounts should be made and shown in the designated place. If you wish more than one officer to endorse checks, you should insert a separate resolution to this effect.

A resolution approving your "Medical Care Reimbursement Plan" should be presented and adopted, if you wish your corporation to pay the medical expenses of the employees and their dependents. Be sure to consult with a tax adviser to assure the tax-free status of this and other corporate fringe benefits (see the discussion in Chapter 4, under "Medical Reimbursement Plans," page 46). A copy of one type of model plan is included in Appendix E.

The next resolution about compensation of officers requires that the officers' salaries be decided upon and shown in the appropriate blanks.

If you wish to elect Subchapter S treatment for your corporation, then a resolution to this effect should be made and included in the minutes. (See Chapter 8, "The S Corporation"). We have included this optional resolution in the minutes. Cross it out if your corporation does not make this election.

Resolutions are also included in the minutes regarding the qualification of common stock as 1244 stock. The purpose of these resolutions is to allow the stockholders of the corporation the benefit of treating losses from the sale, exchange, or worthlessness of their stock as "ordinary" instead of "capital" losses. Since ordinary losses are generally fully deductible whereas long-term capital losses are only 50 percent deductible, it is advantageous to have your stock treated as 1244 stock.

Resolutions concerning the sale and issuance of capital stock are also normally in order. You may fill in the blank showing the number of shares authorized in the Articles of Incorporation. Shares of stock issued for cash are easily entered in the minutes by indicating in the blanks the number of shares purchased and the price of each share. In the case of shares issued for property, the number of shares exchanged for property and the price per share as well as a description of the property are to be shown in the next resolution.

If you are transferring the assets and liabilities of a going business to the corporation in exchange for stock, then you will need to complete the next two resolutions as well. Technically speaking, even if you are the sole owner of a proprietorship and are transferring this business to the corporation, a "Bill of Sale Agreement" should be executed (see Appendix E for a model of this form). The date of the offer of transfer of business, which details the assets and liabilities of the business being transferred, and the fair market value of the business should be indicated in the appropriate blanks.

Finally, the secretary will need to sign the last page of the minutes. A copy of the waiver of notice, a copy of the prepared minutes, a copy of the Articles of Incorporation, a sample copy of the corporation stock certificate (with the word "SPECIMEN" written across the face), a copy of the bank depository resolution form, and any other applicable forms should be placed in the corporate records book. Stock certificates and stubs may be placed in a separate binder or in a special section of the same binder as the other corporate records. Minutes of future meetings of shareholders and directors and all other documents pertaining to the corporation such as loan agreement forms and other legal papers should be filed with the corporate records upon receipt. The corporate records book is required by law to be kept at the principal executive office at all times. In the event of an audit by the IRS or a lawsuit, your corporate records may be subject to close scrutiny. No matter how small your corporation, if you do not keep proper records, you may be subject to various legal and tax penalties.

Issuing Shares of Stock

Once the first meeting of the board of directors is concluded, stock certificates can now be issued in exchange for cash or the assets of a going business. Currently, you do not have to register with the Securities Department stock issued by your corporation that is valued at $100,000 or less or is issued to 35 ore fewer individuals.

Each share certificate can represent any number of shares of stock, the number of shares to be indicated in the upper right-hand corner of the certificate. In addition, each certificate can be issued to more than one person if desired, in the case of husband and wife or other individuals who wish to hold stock jointly with rights of survivorship or as tenants in common or as tenants by the entireties. A sample stock certificate and instructions for filling it out follow hereafter.

Instructions for Filling Out Stock Certificates
If you order a complete corporate outfit like the one advertised in the back of this book, some of the following steps will be completed for you, with custom printing of your company name, state, and the consecutive numbering of the certificates and stubs. First, you fill out the stub portion of the stock certificates, which is either attached directly to the certificates or separate.

Concerning the certificate number to be supplied in the top center space, you will simply number consecutively each certificate to be issued, 1, 2, 3, etc. Be sure that the number on the stub matches the number on the face of the certificate. The stub numbered 1 will be the corporate record of the certificate numbered 1, issued to a particular stockholder, for instance.

Moving down the stub, next indicate the number of shares purchased by that individual and the name of the person to whom issued and fill in the date.

Leave the middle section, "From Whom Transferred," blank. This is used in the case of transfer of the certificate to a new owner.

At the bottom of the stub, you again fill in the certificate number, the number of shares, the date of issuance, and have the stockholder sign on the bottom line.

On the stock certificate proper, indicate the certificate number in the upper left-hand corner and the number of shares represented by the certificate in the upper right-hand corner. Fill in the name of the state in the space under the words "Incorporated Under the Laws of." The upper middle portion of the certificate has a large blank space in which to write the name of the corporation. In the body of the certificate, you may simply fill in the blanks for the owner's name and number of shares. The next blank can be used to indicate the par value of the stock ($10 each, for example). If you have issued no-par value stock, write "no par value" in the blank instead.

In the space for the name of the shareholder, you can, as noted, write in more than one name. If this is done, you would normally put in brackets after the names the type of joint ownership elected, for example: **Junior and Concha Gold, (joint tenants in common**).

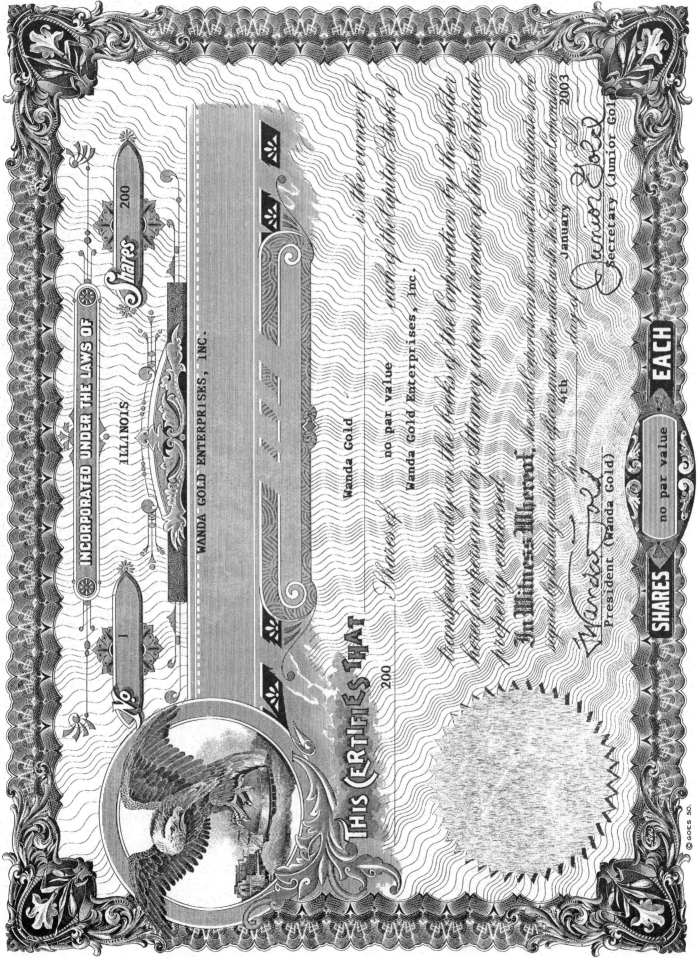

On the right side of the certificate outside the border, you can indicate that your stock issuance conforms with Section 1244 of the Internal Revenue Code for favorable tax treatment, allowing you to deduct corporate losses as an ordinary loss deduction on your personal income tax return (subject to certain limitations). If you choose to have your stock treated as 1244 Stock, you may type the following statement on this portion of the stock certificate:

THESE SHARES ARE ISSUED IN ACCORDANCE WITH SECTION 1244 OF THE INTERNAL REVENUE CODE

An impression of the corporate seal may be made in the gold circular sunburst area at the bottom left side of the certificate.

The date of issuance should also be shown in the place provided. There is space at the bottom of the certificate to type in the names of the corporate officer(s), after each has signed in the appropriate spot.

Each shareholder is given a completed certificate in exchange for cash or the assets of a going business. Stock issued in exchange for cash should be paid for by personal check so that the shareholder will have proof of payment. It is recommended that receipts for cash payments also be issued by the corporation, showing the amount of money received, the check number, the name of the shareholder and the number of shares purchased, the name of the corporation, and the name of the treasurer, as well as the treasurer's signature.

A duplicate copy of each shareholder's receipt should be kept in the share certificate section of the corporate records book. Regarding stock issued in exchange for the assets of a going business, a copy of the signed and dated bill of sale (see Appendix E for this form) will provide documentation of this transaction.

Employer Identification Number

As soon as possible after filing the Articles of Incorporation and selecting a fiscal year for your corporation, you should apply to the IRS for an Employer Identification Number (EIN). You may already have an EIN if you are in business as a sole proprietor. This one won't work, however. You will be required to obtain a new EIN as a corporation.

The form to file is an SS-4, Application for Employer Identification Number. You can phone the IRS and request an SS-4 by snail-mail, or you can download a copy of the form directly from the IRS website (see directory in the back of this book of important addresses, phone numbers, and web addresses). It will usually take 3 to 6 weeks after applying to receive your number by mail. To obtain your EIN immediately in order to file a tax return or make a payment, download the SS-4 from the IRS website, fill out the form, and phone the Tele-TIN number listed for your state under **Where to Apply** (page 2 of the form). An IRS representative will establish an account and assign you an EIN on the spot.

Filing An Assumed Name

There is one more procedure that may or may not apply to your newly formed corporation. Say you incorporate your business under the names of the principals, Unamuno, Grimmelshausen, and Horowitz, Inc. When you are ready to print business cards and stationery, have business signs printed, or run advertisements about your new company, you may have second thoughts about having chosen such a long, cumbersome name, so you decide to call yourselves UGH, Inc. for short.

You must file this "fictitious name" with the Secretary of State. Request a copy of Form BCA-4.15/4.20 from the Illinois Corporation Department and submit it with a $20 fee payment, plus $2.50 for each month between the date of the initial filing and the renewal date. An annual renewal form will be sent to you automatically each year thereafter. Whenever the name under which you do business is different in some way from the one you originally filed when you incorporated, you must follow this procedure. If you operate under the exact corporate name that you filed under, then it is, of course, not necessary to file an assumed name.

Corporate Changes

If you make mistakes of judgment in your original Articles of Incorporation that you later wish to correct, if you wish to change any provision(s) of the original Articles, change your corporate name, convert from a regular to a not for profit corporation, or authorize additional shares of stock, change your status to that of a close corporation, or if the address of your registered office changes, you must notify the Secretary of State of these and similar changes. Contact the Corporation Department for the appropriate form and fee, ranging from $5 for an address change to $25 for a name change and $100 for amending the Articles of Incorporation to authorize additional shares of stock.

Chapter 6. The Illinois Professional Service Corporation and the Illinois Medical Corporation

This chapter will point out certain general characteristics of professional service corporations and discuss specific Illinois laws governing their formation in this state.[1] Professionals who desire to incorporate their practices are strongly advised to use the services of a lawyer.

Professional Liability

As noted in Chapter 1, the owner(s)-operator(s) of an Illinois professional service corporation cannot limit personal liability by means of the "corporate veil" like employees of regular corporations. Nevertheless, professionals who incorporate have more protection from liability than a partnership or sole proprietor.

Although the corporate form does not shield you from personal liability as a professional practitioner in the case of your own malpractice, it does limit your liability as a shareholder of the corporation. If your business goes bankrupt, it does protect your personal assets from creditors. It also provides you with a degree of protection from malpractice on the part of associates (with the exception of incorporated legal firms in Illinois).

Fringe Benefits

Many of the same benefits exist for the professional corporation as for the regular corporation, such as the deductibility of medical and dental expenses and of premiums for medical,

[1] Whereas many states include medical corporations under the broader category of "Professional Service Corporations," Illinois has a separate act governing medical corporations, called "The Medical Corporation Act" (Ch. 32, Pars. 631-648 of the Illinois Revised Statutes). In point of fact, the laws governing medical corporations in the state are virtually the same as those governing professional service corporations. The following discussion will refer to professional service corporations, with the understanding that all statements are equally applicable to medical corporations as well.

disability, and life insurance (up to $50,000 group-term coverage per employee), a $5,000 death benefit, free meals and lodgings furnished for the convenience of the corporation, deductible educational expenses up to $5,250 per employee, employee discounts on goods and services, free parking, group legal services plans, on-site physical fitness facilities, and deductible charitable contributions up to 10 percent of taxable income per year.

Limit on Business Activities

Your professional service corporation cannot engage in any business other than rendering those professional services specifically noted in its Articles. Of course, clerical and technical employees are exceptions to this rule. Your professional corporation may employ these types of workers to render services of a nonprofessional nature. Your professional service corporation is permitted to own stocks, bonds, mortgages, real estate, and other real or personal property. We have already pointed out earlier the tax advantages of corporate vs. individual ownership of passive income-producing property in certain cases (only 30 percent of corporate stock dividends are taxable, for instance). There exists a caveat, however. Corporate capital gains are not capped at a 28 percent rate, like personal income. Instead, they are taxed at the same rate as other income (35 percent in the case of professional service corporations).

Tax Dangers

One aspect of the 1982 federal tax act was especially crucial for personal service corporations. This law permits the IRS to "pierce the corporate veil" in those cases in which a corporation performs substantially all of its services for one other corporation, partnership, or other business entity (for example, a corporation of doctors who all work exclusively for one hospital). In such instances, the IRS now has the power to reallocate income and deductions from the professional service corporation to the individual owners (to the financial detriment of the individuals!). The best way to avoid this problem as an incorporated professional is to make sure that your company provides services to more than one client, whether to several hospitals, clinics or to the public itself. Other devices for assuring the tax-favored status of your professional association can be suggested by a competent legal adviser specializing in this area.

Flat Tax Rate

In the past, professional service corporations enjoyed the same graduated federal corporate tax rates as regular for-profit corporations. This is no longer the case. Professional service corporations involved in activities or services in the fields of health, law, engineering, architecture, accounting, actuarial science, performing arts, and consulting are now taxed at a flat rate of 35 percent (the lower 15 and 25 percent tax brackets are no longer available to these types of corporations). This does not mean that 35 percent of your personal service corporation's income will be paid out to the IRS each year. Only the profits, if any, remaining in the corporation at the end of its tax year will be subject to this flat tax rate. Most personal service corporations accumulate little, or no, profits, however, since their income is largely paid out in deductible salaries, retirement plan contributions, and tax-free fringe benefits. Few personal service corporations will consequently pay substantially more taxes as a result of this tax law change. A tax adviser can help you determine if incorporating your practice will result in an increase in tax liability under your individual circumstances.

Personal service corporations, like regular for-profit corporations, have the option of electing to become S corporations and be taxed at personal federal income tax rates, if this proves advantageous. The major disadvantage of S corporations is that certain fringe benefits are not available to them (See Chapter 8, "The S Corporation").

The procedure whereby you can incorporate your practice, virtually the same for a regular and for-profit corporation, will be outlined below. You will want to weigh the advantages and disadvantages of incorporation and seek the advice of a legal counselor concerning the advisability of such a step in your particular case.

Incorporating as a Professional in Illinois

The Illinois Professional Service Corporation Act authorizes the formation of professional service corporations for the sole purpose of rendering one category of professional services or related services. "Professional service" means any type of professional service which is licensed by the state of Illinois, the U.S. Patent and Trademark Office, or the Internal Revenue Service, including such professional practitioners in Illinois as architects, attorneys, certified or other public accountants, land surveyors, engineers, podiatrists, dentists, and medical practitioners. Related services which are permitted are a combination of two or more professions as defined by Section 3.6 of the Illinois Professional Service Corporation Act (§415-3.6).

Other Powers of Professional Service Corporations

In addition to rendering professional services, professional service corporations are also granted the power to invest their funds in stocks, bonds, real estate, and other forms of investment, and to own real or personal property necessary for rendering professional services. How far a professional service corporation may go in making certain types of investments completely unrelated to its professional practices, for example, the purchase of raw land, is unclear under the present law.

Limits on Mergers or Consolidations
A professional corporation organized in Illinois can consolidate or merge only with another domestic corporation organized under the Professional Service Corporation Act to render the same professional service or services; a merger or consolidation with any foreign corporation is prohibited.

Annual Report Requirement
There exists an annual report requirement for Illinois professional service corporations to assure that non-professionals do not set up and run professional corporations. Each year, every professional service corporation in the state must furnish to the Secretary of State a certificate showing the names and addresses of all shareholders of the corporation and shall certify that all shareholders are duly licensed or otherwise legally authorized in this state to render the same professional service as the corporation. The Secretary of State will automatically send each professional service corporation the required form in advance of the filing deadline. A $40 filing fee is required.

Corporate Organization
The manner of organizing a professional service corporation is basically the same as that of a regular for-profit corporation. A minimum of one incorporator is required, who would be the professional practitioner himself or herself. The Articles of Incorporation for professional service corporations is the same form as that used for general business corporations. A copy of the form (Form BCA-2.10) is included in Appendix A.

Board of Directors
A professional service corporation shall be governed by a board of directors elected by the shareholders and represented by officers elected by the board of directors. If a corporation has only one shareholder, it need have only one director, who shall be such shareholder and may also serve as president, secretary, and treasurer of the corporation. Such one shareholder corporations do not need to have a vice-president. If a corporation has only two shareholders, it need have only two directors, who shall be such shareholders, and they shall fill the offices of president, vice-president, secretary and treasurer of the corporation between them.

Corporate Name
In completing the Articles, the first item, the corporate name, is subject to the provisions of the general corporation law discussed in Chapter 5. The name selected, that is, must be distinguishable from other names of corporations already doing business in Illinois.

The following provisions, in addition, apply to the business names of professional service corporations in Illinois. A professional service corporation shall adopt a name consisting of the full or last name of one or more of its shareholders, except that, if not otherwise prohibited by law, rules of a regulating authority, or the canons of ethics of the profession concerned, a professional service corporation may adopt a fictitious name. If the corporation does adopt a fictitious name or continues to use the name of a shareholder after he or she dies, it shall file the assumed name with the county clerk in accordance with Illinois law. It shall be permissible for a professional service corporation to continue to use the name of a deceased shareholder for a period of one year after his or her death without recording the name of the corporation as an assumed name with the county clerk.

A professional service corporation may also continue to use the name of a shaeholder who voluntarily withdraws from the corporation if the withdrawing shareholder files with the regulating authority his written permission for the continued use of his name by the professional service corporation. This permission shall remain in effect until written revocation has been received by the regulating authority from the former shareholder.

The name of a corporation organized as a professional service corporation must end with one of the following words or abbreviations: "Chartered," "Professional Corporation," "Limited," "Prof. Corp.," "P.C.," or "Ltd."

The name of a medical corporation may either bear the last name of one or more persons formerly or currently associated with it or a fictitious name, provided that the fictitious name is recorded with the county in which it is located. The name must end with one of the following words or abbreviations: "Chartered," "Service Corporation," "Limited," "S.C.," or "Ltd."

Specific Purpose Clause Required in Articles

The purpose clause of the Articles must state the particular professional purpose for which the professional association is being organized. A general purpose clause is *not* acceptable. For example, the following formula or a similar one may be used, filling in the name of the particular profession in the blank:

PROFESSIONAL ASSOCIATION: To practice the profession of _____, rendering that type of professional service and services ancillary thereto.

Professional services will be rendered from the following addresses:

_____
_____
_____

For medical corporations, a specific purpose clause is also required and should be stated as follows:

MEDICAL CORPORATION: To own, operate and maintain an establishment for the study, diagnosis and treatment of human ailments and injuries, whether physical or mental, and to promote medical, surgical, and scientific research and knowledge, provided the medical or surgical treatment, advice or consultation will be given by employees of the corporation only, if they are licensed pursuant to the Medical Practice Act.

Licensing and Certificate Requirement

After your professional corporation is organized, you must then register it with the appropriate regulating authority, either the Department of Professional Regulation (in the case of medical corporations and a number of other professional corporations) or the Clerk of the Illinois Supreme Court (in the case of attorneys). Applications for this purpose are available from the respective officers, whose address and phone number are listed below. A nonrefundable registration fee of $50 is assessed in the case of both medical corporations and professional service corporations. Each incorporator must, of course, be licensed in Illinois to practice the profession for which the corporation is organized.

The corporation must obtain a certificate of registration from the regulating authority that licenses individuals to engage in that particular profession *before* opening and operating an establishment providing medical or other professional services. Illinois professions licensed by the Department of Registration and Education can obtain such certification, by letter or in person, at the following address:

Department of Professional Regulation
320 W. Washington Street, Third Floor
Springfield, Illinois 62786
Telephone (217) 785-0800

Call (217) 782-8556 to verify the details of this procedure and to request an application form. You will need to enclose with the application form (Application for a Medical or Professional Service Corporation License) a photocopy of your Certificate and Articles of Incorporation, a list of all incorporators, shareholders, directors and officers, evidence of filing with the Recorder of Deeds if the corporate name is fictitious, and a $50 check.

Lawyers must obtain a "Certificate of Admission" from the Illinois Supreme Court by filing duplicate copies of a completed Application for Certificate of Registration to Engage in the Practice of Law as a Professional Corporation, along with a check for $50. Contact:

Clerk of the Supreme Court
Supreme Court Building
Springfield, Illinois 62706
Telephone (217) 782-2035

In addition to the above requirement, attorneys must add another statement to the Articles of Incorporation:
All shareholders or members shall be jointly and severally liable for the acts, errors and omissions of the shareholders or members and other employees of the corporation arising out of the performance of professional services by the corporation or association while they are shareholders or members.

Stock Division

The Articles shall provide for the purchase or redemption of the shares of any shareholder upon his death or disqualification; the same may be provided for in the bylaws of the corporation or in a separate agreement. A professional service corporation issues stock subject to the same requirements as a for-profit general corporation. No individual shall hold or any way have an interest in more than one professional service corporation in Illinois.

Chapter 7. The Illinois Not for Profit Corporation

Article 3, Section 103.05 of the Illinois Not for Profit Corporation Act defines a number of purposes for which corporations may be organized under this Act, including:

charitable, benevolent, eleemosynary, educational, civic, patriotic, political, religious, social, literary, athletic, and scientific purposes; various purposes related to agriculture, horticulture, and soil and crop improvement; livestock or poultry improvement; professional, commercial, industrial or trade association; promoting the development, establishment or expansion of industries; electrification on a cooperative basis; telephone service on a mutual or cooperative basis; ownership and operation of water supply facilities for drinking and general domestic use on a mutual or cooperative basis; ownership or administration of residential property on a cooperative basis; administration and operation of a co-op; a condominium association, or a homeowner association; operation of a community mental health board or center organized pursuant to the "Community Mental Health Act" for the purpose of providing direct patient services; provision of consumer credit counseling as authorized by the "Consumer Credit Counseling Corporation Act;

promotion, operation, and administration of a ridesharing arrangement; administration and operation of an organization for the purpose of assisting low-income consumers in the acquisition of utility and telephone services.

As you can see, a wide variety of corporations, from those organized to run political campaigns to those engaged in humanitarian endeavors— from 4H clubs to religious societies— may be formed under this section. Condominium associations are also organized under this section.

In spite of its nonprofit purpose, employees of a not for profit corporation are entitled to draw a reasonable salary for services rendered to the corporation, but neither they nor the directors or members can take earnings out of the corporation in the form of dividends or other personal benefits.

Not for Profit Articles of Incorporation

An Illinois not for profit corporation is similar in certain respects to an Illinois profit corporation but different in others. As in the case of a profit corporation, Articles of Incorporation must be filed with the Secretary of State in order to set up the corporate entity. A copy of the not for profit Articles is included in Appendix E.

Articles of Incorporation of a not for profit corporation shall be executed and filed in duplicate and shall set forth:

(1) The name of the corporation.
(2) The *specific* purpose or purposes for which the corporation is organized. It shall not be sufficient to state substantially that the corporation may engage in any activity within the purposes for which a corporation may be organized under this act (a general purpose clause may *not* be used, as in the case of a corporation organized under the Illinois Business Corporation Act, in other words). You can use everyday language to describe the purpose(s) of your proposed not for profit corporaton, for example: "To set up a shelter for abandoned dogs and cats." "To administer and operate a condominium association." Or "To run a political campaign with the purpose of getting John Doe elected governor of the state of Illinois."

⇒**If your corporation is applying for tax-exempt status with the Internal Revenue Service, the language required for exempt status should be included in your purpose clause. In addition to the standard language required by the IRS for exempt status, you will also need to spell out the specific purposes of your proposed corporation in order to meet the requirements of Illinois law.** [1]

(3) The address of the corporation's initial registered office and the name of the corporation's initial registered agent at that office.
(4) The name and address of each incorporator.
(5) The number of directors constituting the first board of directors and the names and the residential addresses of each such director. A minimum of three directors is required for an Illinois not for profit corporation.
(6) With respect to any organization a purpose of which is to function as a club, as defined in Section 1-3.24 of "The Liquor Control Act of 1934," as now or hereafter amended, a statement that it will comply with the state and local laws and ordinances relating to alcoholic beverages.
(7) Whether the corporation is a condominium, a cooperative housing corporation, or a homeowner association.

In addition to the *required* information listed above that *must* appear in the Articles of Incorporation of a not for profit corporation, the Articles may also set forth:

(1) The names of any persons or the designation of any group of persons who are to be the initial members.
(2) Any qualifications of membership and the classification of members.
(3) A provision to the effect that the corporation shall be subordinate to and subject to the authority of any head or national association, lodge, order, beneficial association, fraternal or beneficial society, foundation, federation, or any other non-profit corporation, society, organization, or association.
(4) Any lawful provision for the purpose of defining, limiting, or regulating the exercise of the authority of the corporation, the incorporators, the directors, the officers, the members, or any class of members, or creating or defining rights and privileges of the members among themselves or in the property of the corporation, or governing the distribution of assets on dissolution.
(5) Any provision that may be set forth in the corporate bylaws.
(6) A provision superseding any provision of the Not for Profit Corporation Act that requires for approval of corporate action a two-thirds vote of members by allowing any smaller or larger vote requirement (but not less than a majority).
(7) A provision specifying the period of existence of the corporation if it is to be otherwise than perpetual.

All of these optional provisions may be set forth in the corporate bylaws instead of the Articles of Incorporation if you so choose.

---

[1] Tax-exempt status is not obtained by filing not for profit Articles of Incorporation with the Secretary of State. You must apply to the IRS for tax-exempt status. See IRS Publication 587, "Tax Exempt Status for Your Organization."

Names of Not for Profit Corporations

The Secretary of State will not accept any name for a not for profit corporation that implies that the corporation is organized for any purpose other than a purpose for which corporations may be organized under this Act, or a purpose other than the purpose set forth in its Articles of Incorporation. The name of a not for profit corporation *may* contain the word "corporation," "company," "incorporated," or "limited," or an abbreviation of one such word. As in the case of profit corporations, the name must be distinguishable from the corporate name of any other domestic or foreign corporation, whether profit or not for profit, already doing business in the state of Illinois. The name of a not for profit corporation shall not contain the words "democrat," "republican," nor the name of any other established political party, unless consent to usage of such words or name is given to the corporation by the state central committee of such established political party.

A not for profit corporation, like a profit corporation, may choose to adopt an assumed corporate name. See page 75 for a discussion of the procedure for filing an assumed name in Illinois.

The same procedures for reserving a corporate name or checking the availability of a proposed name by telephone may be followed as those for a profit corporation (see Chapter 5, pages 53-55). In order to reserve a name, you must pay a fee of $25 and submit the appropriate form (see the Name Reservation form BCA-4.10 in Appendix E).

Registered Office and Registered Agent

Like a profit corporation, a not for profit corporation must also maintain a registered office (which may be the same as its place of business) and a registered agent. This agent may be anyone who is a resident of Illinois, including, but not limited to, one of the incorporators of the corporation. See the discussion of the registered agent's role in Chapter 5, page 58.

Corporate Bylaws

As in the case of a profit corporation, other documents internal to the organization of the corporation, such as the corporate bylaws, are *not* filed with the Secretary of State. After the filing and approval of the Articles by the Secretary of State, the board of directors shall adopt bylaws for the regulation and management of the corporation. Bylaws would cover such issues as:

- the time and place for holding and the manner of conducting meetings
- qualifications for membership and its determination
- fees and dues of members
- the rights of members
- various points concerning the number, qualifications, compensation, and removal of officers
- method of changing the bylaws

Section 107 of the Illinois Not for Profit Corporation Act provides guidelines and requirements for writing the bylaws for those corporations organized on a membership basis.

Powers of Not for Profit Corporations

The specific authority of not for profit corporations, which enjoy basically the same powers as profit corporations, is spelled out in Section 103.10 of the Not for Profit Corporation Act.

See the section on "Powers of Profit Corporations" in Chapter 2 (pages 24-25). Not for profit corporations possess these same powers. These powers include such rights as the right to sue and be sued, to have and affix a corporate seal, to make contracts and incur liabilities, to elect or appoint officers, to make and alter bylaws, to loan money for its corporate purposes, and so on.

Membership Book, Minutes, Meeting Notices, Officers' Terms, Quorums, Amendments to Articles, and Voluntary Dissolution

The not for profit corporation is required to keep a membership book with a record giving the name and address of each member entitled to vote. In addition, it must maintain correct and complete books and records of account as well as minutes of the proceedings of its members, board of directors, and committees having any of the authority of the board of directors. Specific requirements of the Not for Profit Corporation Act also govern such matters as how much advance notice members must be given of meetings (not less than five nor more than 60 days' notice); meetings of directors (to be prescribed in the bylaws); directors' terms of office (one year unless staggered); quorums for meetings (a majority unless the Articles or bylaws provide otherwise); amendments to Articles of Incorporation; and voluntary dissolution.

Major Differences Between Profit and Not for Profit Corporations

The major differences from a profit corporation in the filing of Articles of Incorporation include the following:

(a) A specific not for profit purpose must be stated in the Articles of Incorporation of a not for profit corporation.
(b) The name of the corporation does not require a corporate ending, such as "inc.," "corporation," or "co."
(c) The corporation must be organized on a nonstock basis.
(d) A statement must indicate whether the corporation is to be organized on a membership basis (as in the case of a fraternal organization) or on a directorial basis (as in the case of certain charitable organizations).

(e) The filing fee for a not for profit Articles of Incorporation is $50.

Other Requirements

Recording the Articles
As in the case of Articles for profit corporations, once you have received the Articles and accompanying Certificate back from the Secretary of State you must file them with the Recorder of Deeds of the county in which the registered office of the corporation is located within 15 days of receipt.

Applying for an EIN
Your not for profit corporation will also need to apply for a Federal Employer Identification Number. See page 74 for an explanation of the procedure.

Corporations Involved in the Solicitation of Funds
Any not for profit corporation (as well as profit corporation) involved in the solicitation of funds for charitable purposes will need to register with the Division of Charitable Trust and Solicitations of the Attorney General. Information and forms can be obtained from:

Illinois Attorney General
Division of Charitable Trust and Solicitations
100 West Randolph, 3rd floor
Chicago, Illinois 60601
Telephone (312) 814-2595

Filing of Federal and State Income Tax Returns
If you receive tax-exempt status from the IRS, as discussed below, you will not need to file federal or Illinois state income tax returns. If you are not tax-exempt, you will need to file in each case.

Exemption from Illinois Sales Tax
Some not for profit corporations may qualify for an exemption from paying Illinois sales tax on goods bought for the use of their organization if it is formed for exclusively charitable, religious or educational purposes or exclusively for the benefit of senior citizens. If you fit into one of these categories, write a letter of request to the Illinois Department of Revenue, Sales Tax Division. Enclose photocopies of your Articles of Incorporation, your corporate bylaws, constitution, IRS exemption letter or any other document that may assist the Sales Tax Division to determine your status. The Division will rule on your status as soon as possible. If you qualify for sales tax exemption, a letter ruling will be sent to you notifying you to that effect. Write to:

Illinois Department of Revenue
Sales Tax Division
101 West Jefferson
Springfield, Illinois 62708
Telephone 1-800-732-8866

Operation Under an Assumed Name

A not for profit corporation may also operate under an assumed name, by registering the true and assumed names with the Secretary of State. The appropriate form (BCA-4.15/20) is available from the Secretary of State. The fee for registering an assumed name is $20 plus $2.50 for each month between the date of the initial filing and the renewal date.

Applying for Tax-Exempt Status

Some not for profit corporations are entitled to tax-exempt status, and others are not. Tax-exempt status is *not* obtained by filing not for profit Articles of Incorporation with the Illinois Secretary of State. You must apply to the Internal Revenue Service for tax-exempt status. Consult IRS Publication 587, "Tax-exempt Status for Your Organization" concerning the application procedure. In general, if your organization falls under one of the following purposes, it is *not* eligible for tax-exempt status: athletic, benevolent, eleemosynary, and social.

Tax-exempt status is granted by the IRS under a particular section of the IRS Code, section 501(c)(3). Organizations qualifying for tax-exempt status are often referred to as 501(c)(3) organizations. If your organization falls under this section of the IRS Code, as explained in Publication 587, the

language required for exempt status should be included in the purpose clause of your Articles of Incorporation. In addition to the standard language required by the IRS for exempt status, you will also need to spell out the *specific* purposes of your proposed corporation in order to meet the requirements of Illinois law.

Chapter 8. The S Corporation

An S corporation is a special "small business corporation" that has no more than 75 shareholders.[1] This form of operation is normally adopted by relatively small businesses, but larger firms can also elect S status as long as they meet the limitation on the number of shareholders. The 1981 and 1982 tax acts and the Subchapter S Revision Act of 1982 made S corporations easier to form and operate. Consequently, the number of such corporations increased dramatically over the past two decades. Some of the tax advantages of S corporations were reduced under the Clinton tax act. As a result, this form of business operation is no longer as advantageous for certain individuals, particularly ones in the highest tax brackets.[2] It remains to be seen if the pending tax changes under the new Bush administration will once again restore the advantages of S corporation formation for high-income individuals.

If a business anticipates large start-up losses in the early years of operation, an S corporation may be advisable. In the past, very profitable businesses also had an advantage when they operated as an S corporation. This was the case because the highest personal tax rate was lower than the highest corporate tax rate, and, as we shall see, the income from S corporations is taxed at the personal rate(s) of the owner(s) of the company. These two situations, the business with start-up losses and the highly profitable business, will be considered in depth below.

If you plan to elect S status, consultation with an attorney is recommended, especially with the recent advent of a new type of business entity taxed exactly like an S corporation, the limited liability company.

Structure of S Corporations

The S corporation is like a partnership in that it pays no federal taxes in itself.[3] Instead, the income of the corporation is divided in proportion to the stock holdings of the shareholders and is taxed to them as individuals. Likewise, corporate losses are not deducted by the corporation but are passed through directly to the shareholders, who can use the deductions—generally in the year the loss occurs—to offset income from other sources. Like the partnership

---

[1] For years, the number of shareholders of an S corporation was limited to 35, but a recent change in the law has raised this figure to 75.
[2] 36 percent and 39.6 percent. Under the new Bush tax laws, all tax bracket rates will be gradually reduced starting in the year 2002.

[3] The state of Illinois currently taxes Subchapter S corporations at the rate of 1.5 percent of net income and requires the filing of Form IL-1120-ST.

tax return, the S federal tax return (Form 1120S) is an informational return listing the names of the shareholders and their pro rata share of profits or losses.

Six Requirements for S Status

A corporation can elect S status by the written consent of all the stockholders, provided it meets six requirements:

1. It must be a domestic corporation (i.e., one located anywhere in the United States).
2. None of the shareholders may be non-resident aliens.
3. There must be no more than 75 shareholders. Shares held in joint ownership by husband and wife (and their estates) are counted as one shareholder.
4. The corporation can't be a member of a group of affiliated corporations (certain corporations which own stock in other corporations are defined by the IRS as "affiliated").
5. There must be only one class of stock, with all shares having equal rights (differences in regard to voting rights *alone* are permitted, however, allowing for voting and non-voting shares, if desired).
6. Banks that use the reserve method of accounting for bad debts, insurance companies subject to tax under the rules of subchapter L, and certain other specialized types of corporations are prohibited from electing S status.

IRS Publication 589 gave more detailed information concerning S election and other special rules governing S corporations. It has been inexplicably discontinued. This chapter will cover the main highlights of S election. If more detailed information is required, phone the IRS Taxpayer Assistance line listed in the phone and address directory provided in the back of this book.

Advantage of Voting and Non-Voting Stock

In the past, you were barred from adopting S status if your corporation had both voting and non-voting stock. As pointed out in Chapter 2, the Subchapter S Revision Act of 1982 eliminated this requirement. The creation of non-voting as well as voting stock is now permitted, provided that both voting and non-voting stock is equal in all other respects regarding rights and limitations. This provision makes it very easy to lower taxes by shifting income to family members in lower tax brackets.

By giving non-voting, dividend-paying stock to retired parents or children while keeping voting stock in the hands of the directors of the corporation, you will ease your tax burden without sacrificing control of the company. You do not have to adopt S status in order for your corporation to have both voting and non-voting stock, of course. A regular corporation can have both voting and non-voting stock as well. The point is that S corporations and regular corporations are now on an equal footing in this area, which was not the case in the past.

Applying to the IRS for S Status

Application for S status is made by completing Form 2553. This form is available from the IRS and must be filed at any time on or before the 15th day of the third month of the corporation's tax year or any time during the preceding tax year. For newly formed corporations that wish to begin life as S corporations, this will generally mean filing Form 2553 within 75 days of the date of incorporation. In the event that the IRS later claims non-receipt of the form, it (as well as other important documents with deadlines) should be sent via certified mail with return receipt requested. This will verify both the mailing and the postmarked date and will stand up in court in the event of any dispute. All the current shareholders of the corporation must agree to the S election, as well as all persons who were shareholders during the taxable year before the election was made.

Fiscal Year of S Corporations

The fiscal year of newly formed S corporations is now required to be a calendar year (January 1 to December 31) unless there is a business purpose for a fiscal year other than the calendar one.

Revocation of S Status

If stockholders representing a majority of the stock of the corporation file shareholder consents to revocation, S status can be terminated in any successive years. Five years must elapse before you can switch back to S status, however, unless the IRS consents to an earlier re-election. Your S status can also be revoked by the IRS for infringement of the requirements, for instance, if you issue a second class of stock, increase the number of shareholders to more than 75, and so on. Since it may take several years before the IRS discovers that some violation in the past has voided your S status, a thorough familiarity with the laws governing S corporations is a must. There are other times when it may prove beneficial to the corporation to initiate some action in order deliberately to have its S status revoked.

S Election for Businesses Losing Money

There exist distinct advantages for some individuals in operating an S corporation. If your business is losing money in the first year or two, it may be very beneficial to be able to deduct these losses directly from your personal income tax return, up to the amount of your basis in the stock of the corporation. In a regular corporation, you have the right to carry these losses forward and deduct them from corporate income in future years when the company is realizing a profit, subject to certain restrictions.

Once the S corporation begins to show a profit, earnings will be taxed at individual shareholder, not corporate, rates. At this point, you may choose to terminate the election and revert to a regular corporation or stay as an S, depending on your individual circumstances. If your corporate tax bracket would be lower than your personal tax bracket, then a regular corporation will be advantageous, from the point of view of taxes. On the other hand, if your personal tax bracket is lower than the corporation's, an S corporation will allow you to funnel your business income to yourself at lower tax rates. Given the complexity of this issue at present, owing to the current changes in the tax laws, consultation with a tax adviser is highly recommended if you are considering organizing your business as an S corporation.

S Corporation as Family Tax Shelter

As noted previously, S corporations work well as "family tax shelters," since business owners with children or other relatives (on friendly terms!) can issue non-voting, dividend-paying stock to their dependents or relations and keep income within the family at lower personal tax rates. With the Clinton 1993 tax act, the main issue became, Will personal tax rates in your individual case be lower than corporate rates, or higher? This is no longer a

clear-cut issue for many S corporate owners or potential owners, given the present changes and proposed changes in the tax brackets. For the single owner without dependents, a regular corporation may sometimes prove more favorable taxwise, but this may change as the individual and business tax rates change under the Bush administration.

S Format for Profitable Business

In a very profitable business in which dividends have to be issued to escape the IRS's "accumulated earnings penalty," it may very well be advantageous to avoid double taxation on dividends at both the corporate and individual level by opting for S status and paying out all the earnings of the business each year. This tax strategy will work best for small corporations that are profitable, particularly those with large families in which the income can be parceled out among a number of different family members. The windfall dividends may kick you into the highest personal tax bracket. But the tax savings from avoiding double taxation will ordinarily more than offset this disadvantage.

With an S corporation, you are more or less required to distribute all the profits of the corporation within two and one-half months of the end of the tax year or suffer severe tax penalties. Profits not so distributed are considered "constructive dividends" by the IRS and taxed to you individually even though they remain in the corporation.

Obviously, the S arrangement will not work well for capital-intensive businesses that need to accumulate earnings for large capital expenditures on a regular basis, unless the company is prepared to issue bonds or resort to similar measures to raise needed capital. Generally speaking, a corporation that can pay out virtually all its earnings each year through a combination of deductible expenses (such as salaries, pension plan contributions, and so on) and dividends will function well as an S. For others, there may be potential problems and tax penalties in the case of undistributed income that is "locked in" the S corporation. This is a complicated area, so plan to consult a tax adviser if you are considering forming an S corporation.

Pension Plans of S Corporations; Fringe Benefits

One previous disadvantage of this form of operation was the much smaller pension plan contributions allowable for S corporations, compared to regular corporations. Many of these differences have now been eliminated. On the minus side, the new law makes previously tax-free medical and life insurance benefits taxable to shareholders who own more than 2 percent of the corporation's stock. In other words, there is a trade-off. In exchange for the lower tax rates

available under certain circumstances to S corporation owners, you lose the opportunity to receive certain tax-free employee fringe benefits.

New Ceiling on Passive Income

The tax law has made S status attractive for certain groups formerly barred from election, such as investment companies and real estate firms and other businesses that typically have large passive income from interest, dividends, annuities, rents, royalties, and gains from sales or exchanges of stock and securities. In the past, S status was denied to companies whose passive income exceeded 20 percent of gross receipts. Since 1983, the ceiling on passive income has been raised from 20 to 25 percent. Even if a company exceeds this limit, its election will not be terminated if the corporation pays a tax of 46 percent of the passive income in excess of the 25 percent of gross receipts. Most importantly, any unincorporated business that becomes an S corporation under the new law or any business that has had S status since it originally incorporated can now receive unlimited passive income.

Pass-throughs in Like Kind

Another major advantage of the revamped S corporation is that capital gains and tax-exempt income of the company will be passed through to the shareholders in like kind. That is, it will remain taxable at capital gains rates[4] or be tax-free, as the case may be, whereas in the past all such distributions were treated and taxed as ordinary dividend income to the shareholders.

Other Tax Advantages

Several other tax advantages of the S corporation center on the treatment of capital gains and net operating losses. In the past, an owner of a company with a net operating loss exceeding the owner's capital investment could not deduct the amount in excess of the owner's "tax basis." This excess amount can now be carried forward and deducted in future years against corporate profits, provided the owner puts additional capital into the corporation equal to the excess loss deducted. Also, shareholders can now report the net operating losses and capital gains of the corporation separately, whereas in the past the two had to be used to offfset each other. For S corporations with capital gains and net operating losses, this can mean a substantial tax savings.

Resolutions to Adopt S Status

After weighing the pros and cons, if you choose to organize your business as an S corporation, resolutions to this effect should be included in the Minutes of the First Meeting of the Board of Directors (see Appendix D). For example,

RESOLVED, that the corporation elect to be treated as a "Small Business Corporation" for income tax purposes under Subchapter S of the Internal Revenue Code.

RESOLVED FURTHER, that the officers of this corporation be and hereby are authorized and directed to obtain the written consent of the shareholders to the foregoing election and to file Form 2553 with the IRS.

These two resolutions to adopt S status have, in fact, already been included in the sample Minutes of the First Meeting of the Board of Directors in Appendix D. If you choose not to elect S status, these two resolutions should be crossed out.

---

[4] For tax year 1999 and thereafter, the top capital gains rate is 20 percent on long-term gains from assets held more than 12 months.

APPENDIX A

Articles of Incorporation for Profit Corporations (Including Professional Service Corporations)

Form **BCA-2.10** | **ARTICLES OF INCORPORATION**

(Rev. Jan. 1999)

Jesse White
Secretary of State
Department of Business Services
Springfield, IL 62756
http://www.sos.state.il.us

Payment must be made by certified check, cashier's check, Illinois attorney's check, Illinois
C.P.A's check or money order,
payable to "Secretary of State."

This space for use by Secretary of State

SUBMIT IN DUPLICATE!

This space for use by Secretary of State

Date

Franchise Tax $

Filing Fee $

Approved:

---

1. CORPORATE NAME: _____

    _____

    (The corporate name must contain the word "corporation", "company," "incorporated," "limited" or an abbreviation thereof.)

---

2. Initial Registered Agent: _____

    First Name   *Middle Initial*   *Last name*

    Initial Registered Office: _____

    Number   *Street*   *Suite #*

    _____ IL _____

    City   *County*   *Zip Code*

---

3. Purpose or purposes for which the corporation is organized:
    (If not sufficient space to cover this point, add one or more sheets of this size.)

---

4. Paragraph 1: Authorized Shares, Issued Shares and Consideration Received:

Class	Par Value per Share	Number of Shares Authorized	Number of Shares Proposed to be Issued	Consideration to be Received Therefor
	$			$

TOTAL = $

Paragraph 2: The preferences, qualifications, limitations, restrictions and special or relative rights in respect of the shares of each class are:
(If not sufficient space to cover this point, add one or more sheets of this size.)

(over)

5. *OPTIONAL:*   (a) Number of directors constituting the initial board of directors of the corporation:_____ .

                    (b) Names and addresses of the persons who are to serve as directors until the first annual meeting of shareholders or until their successors are elected and qualify:

Name	Residential Address	City, State, ZIP

6. *OPTIONAL:*   (a) It is estimated that the value of all property to be owned by the corporation for the following year wherever located will be: $_____

                    (b) It is estimated that the value of the property to be located within the State of Illinois during the following year will be: $_____

                    (c) It is estimated that the gross amount of business that will be transacted by the corporation during the following year will be: $_____

                    (d) It is estimated that the gross amount of business that will be transacted from places of business in the State of Illinois during the following year will be: $_____

7. *OPTIONAL:*   *OTHER PROVISIONS*

                    Attach a separate sheet of this size for any other provision to be included in the Articles of Incorporation, e.g., authorizing preemptive rights, denying cumulative voting, regulating internal affairs, voting majority requirements, fixing a duration other than perpetual, etc.

8.   **NAME(S) & ADDRESS(ES) OF INCORPORATOR(S)**

The undersigned incorporator(s) hereby declare(s), under penalties of perjury, that the statements made in the foregoing Articles of Incorporation are true.

Dated _____ , _____
                  (Month & Day)   *Year*

Signature and Name	**Address**
1. _____	1. _____
Signature	*Street*
_____	_____
(Type or Print Name)	*City/Town* *State* *ZIP Code*
2. _____	2. _____
Signature	*Street*
_____	_____
(Type or Print Name)	*City/Town* *State* *ZIP Code*
3. _____	3. _____
Signature	*Street*
_____	_____
(Type or Print Name)	*City/Town* *State* *ZIP Code*

(Signatures must be in **BLACK INK** on original document. Carbon copy, photocopy or rubber stamp signatures may only be used on conformed copies.)

NOTE: If a corporation acts as incorporator, the name of the corporation and the state of incorporation shall be shown and the execution shall be by its president or vice president and verified by him, and attested by its secretary or assistant secretary.

FEE SCHEDULE

- The initial franchise tax is assessed at the rate of 15/100 of 1 percent ($1.50 per $1,000) on the paid-in capital represented in this state, with a minimum of $25.
- The filing fee is $75.
- The **minimum total due** (franchise tax + filing fee) is **$100.**
  (Applies when the Consideration to be Received as set forth in Item 4 does not exceed $16,667)
- The Department of Business Services in Springfield will provide assistance in calculating the total fees if necessary.
  Illinois Secretary of State   Springfield, IL 62756
  Department of Business Services   Telephone (217) 782-9522 or 782-9523

C-162.20

APPENDIX B

Bylaws

BYLAWS

of

_____

ARTICLE I
Location

The principal executive office of the corporation in the State of Illinois shall be located in the City/Village of _____ and County of _____. The corporation may have such other offices, either within or without the State of Illinois, as the board of directors may from time to time determine or the business of the corporation may require.

ARTICLE II
Shareholders

Section 1. Place of Meetings. Meetings of the shareholders shall be held at the principal executive office of the corporation or at such other place, within or without the State of Illinois, as the board of directors shall determine.

Section 2. Annual Meeting. The annual meeting of the shareholders shall be held on the _____ day of _____ at _____ A.M./P.M. in each year, for the purpose of electing directors and for the transaction of such additional business as necessary. If the day fixed for the annual meeting shall be a legal holiday, the meeting shall be held on the next succeeding business day at the same hour. If the election of directors shall not be held on the day designated herein for any annual meeting, the board of directors shall cause the election to be held at a meeting of the shareholders as soon thereafter as possible.

Section 3. Special Meetings. Special meetings of the shareholders may be called by the president, by the board of directors, or by the holders of not less than one-fifth of all the outstanding shares of the corporation.

Section 4. Notice of Meetings. Written notice stating the place, date, and hour of meetings shall be delivered not less than ten nor more than sixty days before the date of the meeting, either personally or by mail, by or at the direction of the president, or the secretary, or the officer or persons calling the meeting, to each shareholder of record entitled to vote at such meeting. In the case of a special meeting, the purpose or purposes for which the meeting is called shall be included in the notice. In the case of an annual meeting, those matters which the board at the time of the mailing of the notice intends to present for action by the shareholders (but subject to the provision that any proper matter may be presented at the meeting for such action) shall be set forth. If mailed, the notice is given when deposited in the United States mail, with postage thereon prepaid, directed to the shareholder at his address as it appears on the records of the corporation.

Section 5. Meeting of All Shareholders. If all of the shareholders shall meet at any place and time, either within or without the State of Illinois, and consent to the holding of a meeting at such place and time, such meeting shall be valid without call or notice, and at such meeting any corporate action may be taken.

Section 6. Closing of Transfer Books and Fixing of Record Date. For the purpose of determining shareholders entitled to notice of or to vote at any meeting of the shareholders, or shareholders entitled to receive payment of any dividend, or in order to make a determination of shareholders for any other purpose, the board of directors shall provide that the share transfer books be closed for a stated period but not to exceed, in any case, sixty days. If the share transfer books shall be closed for the purpose of determining shareholders entitled to notice of or to vote at a meeting of shareholders, such books shall be closed for at least ten days, or in the case of a merger, consolidation, share exchange, dissolution, or sale, lease or exchange of assets, not less than twenty days, immediately preceding such meeting. If no record date is fixed for the determination of shareholders entitled to notice of or to vote at a meeting of shareholders, or shareholders entitled to receive payment of a dividend, the date on which notice of the meeting is mailed or the date on which the resolution of the board of directors declaring such dividend is adopted, as the case may be, shall be the record date for such determination of shareholders.

Section 7. Voting Lists. (1) The officer or agent having charge of the stock transfer books for shares of a corporation shall make, within twenty days after the record date for a meeting of shareholders or ten days before such meeting, whichever is earlier, and certify a complete list of the shareholders entitled to vote at a shareholders' meeting or any adjournment thereof. The list shall:

    (a) Be arranged alphabetically within each class and series, with the address of, and the number of shares held by, each shareholder.

    (b) Be kept on file at the registered office of the corporation and be subject to inspection by any shareholder, and to copying at the shareholder's expense, at any time during usual business hours, for a period of ten days prior to such meeting.

    (c) Be produced at the time and place of the meeting.

    (d) Be subject to inspection by any shareholder during the whole time of the meeting.

    (e) Be *prima facie* evidence as to who are the shareholders entitled to examine the list or to vote at the meeting.

(2) If the requirements of this section have not been complied with, on demand of a shareholder in person or by proxy, who in good faith challenges the existence of sufficient votes to carry any action at the meeting, the meeting shall be adjourned until the requirements are complied with. Failure to comply with the requirements of this section does not affect the validity of an action taken at the meeting before the making of such a demand.

An officer or agent having charge of the transfer books who shall fail to prepare the list of shareholders, or keep the same on file for a period of ten days, or produce and keep the same open for inspection at the meeting, as provided in this Section, shall be liable to any shareholder suffering damage on account of such failure, to the extent of the damage.

Section 8. Quorum of Shareholders and Voting by Shareholders. Unless a greater or lesser quorum is provided in the Articles of Incorporation, a majority of the outstanding shares, represented in person or by proxy, constitute a quorum at a meeting of shareholders, but in no event shall a quorum consist of less than one-third of the outstanding shares. If a quorum is present, the affirmative vote of the majority of the shares represented at the meeting and entitled to vote on a matter shall be the act of the shareholders, unless the vote of a greater number or voting by classes is required by The Business Corporation Act or the Articles of Incorporation. The Articles of Incorporation may require any number or percent greater than a majority up to and including the requirement of unanimity to constitute a quorum.

Section 9. Voting of Shares. Subject to the provisions of Section 12 of this Article, each outstanding share, regardless of class, shall be entitled to one vote upon each matter submitted at a meeting of shareholders, unless the Articles of Incorporation provide otherwise. The Articles of Incorporation may limit or deny voting rights or may provide special voting rights as to any class or classes or series of shares of the corporation.

Section 10. Proxies. At all meetings of shareholders, a shareholder may vote either in person or by proxy executed in writing by the shareholder or by his duly authorized agent or representative. No proxy shall be valid after 11 months from the date of its execution, unless otherwise provided in the proxy.

Section 11. Voting of Shares by Certain Holders. Shares standing in the name of another corporation--domestic or foreign--may be voted by such officer, agent, or proxy as the Bylaws of such corporation may prescribe, or, in the absence of such provision, as the board of directors of such corporation may determine.

Shares of its own stock belonging to this corporation shall not be voted, directly or indirectly, at any meeting and shall not be counted in determining the total number of outstanding shares entitled to vote at any given time, but shares of its own stock held by it in a fiduciary capacity may be voted and shall be counted in determining the total number of outstanding shares entitled to vote at any given time.

Shares standing in the name of a receiver may be voted by such receiver, and shares held by or under the control of a receiver may be voted by such receiver without the transfer thereof into his name if authority so to do is contained in an appropriate order of the court by which such receiver was appointed.

Shares standing in the name of a deceased person, a minor ward or a person under legal disability, may be voted by his administrator, executor, court-appointed guardian or conservator, either in person or by proxy without a transfer of shares into the name of such administrator, executor, court-appointed guardian or conservator. Shares standing in the name of a trustee may be voted by him, either in person or by proxy.

A shareholder whose shares are pledged shall be entitled to vote such shares until the shares have been transferred into the name of the pledgee, and thereafter the pledgee shall be entitled to vote the shares so transferred.

Section 12. Cumulative Voting. Unless specifically limited or eliminated by the Articles of Incorporation, .every shareholder in an election for directors shall exercise cumulative voting rights. In so doing, each shareholder shall have the right to vote, in person or by proxy, the number of shares owned by him, for as many persons as there are directors to be elected, or to cumulate said shares, and give one candidate as many votes as the number of directors multiplied by the number of his shares shall equal, or to distribute them on the same principle among as many candidates as he shall think fit.

Section 13. Inspectors. At any meeting of shareholders, the chairman of the meeting may, or upon the request of any shareholder shall, appoint one or more persons as inspectors for such meeting.

Such inspectors shall ascertain and report the number of shares represented at the meeting, the existence of a quorum, and the validity and effect of proxies; count all votes and report the results; and do such other acts as are proper to conduct the election and voting with impartiality and fairness to all the shareholders.

Each report of an inspector shall be in writing and signed by him or by a majority of them if there be more than one inspector acting at such meeting. If there is more than one inspector, the report of a majority shall be the report of the inspectors. The report of the inspector or inspectors on the number of shares represented at the meeting and the results of the voting shall be *prima facie* evidence thereof.

Section 14. Action without Meeting. Any action which may be taken at any annual or special meeting of shareholders may be taken without a meeting and without prior notice if a consent in writing setting forth the action so taken shall be signed by the holders of all the outstanding shares entitled to vote or signed by such lesser number of holders as may be provided for in the Articles of Incorporation that would be necessary to authorize or take such action at a meeting.

ARTICLE III
Directors

Section 1. Powers. Subject to any provision in the Articles of Incorporation, including the stipulation that the corporation be run under a shareholders' agreement according to the Close Corporation Act of 1977, the business and affairs of the corporation shall be managed by a board of directors.

Section 2. Number. The authorized number of directors shall be _____ until changed by amendment to this Article of these Bylaws.

Section 3. Election and Term of Directors. Each director shall hold office until the next annual meeting of shareholders or until his successor shall have been elected and qualified, or until his prior resignation or removal. Unless otherwise provided in the Articles of Incorporation, a director may be removed, with or without cause, by vote of the holders of a majority of the shares entitled to vote at an election of directors, subject to Section 8.35 of the Business Corporation Act. Directors need not be residents of Illinois or shareholders of the corporation unless the Articles so prescribe.

Section 4. Vacancies. Any vacancy occurring in the board of directors and any directorship to be filled by reason of an increase in the number of directors may be filled by election at an annual meeting or at a special meeting of shareholders called for that purpose. A director elected to fill a vacancy shall serve until the next annual meeting of shareholders at which directors are to be elected.

Section 5. Regular Meetings. A regular meeting of the board of directors shall be held without other notice than this Bylaw, immediately after and at the same place as the annual meeting of shareholders. The board of directors may provide, by resolution, the time and place, for the holding of additional regular meetings without other notice than this resolution.

Section 6. Manner of Convening Special Meetings. Special meetings of the board of directors may be called by or at the request of the president or any two directors.

Section 7. Place of Special Meetings. The person or persons authorized to convene special meetings of the board of directors may fix any place, either within or without the State of Illinois, as the place for holding any special meeting of the board of directors.

Section 8. Notice of Directors' Meetings. Special meetings of the board of directors shall be held upon at least four days' prior notice in writing, delivered personally or mailed to the business address of each director. Any director may waive notice of any meeting. Attendance of a director at any meeting shall constitute a waiver of notice of such meeting except where a director attends a meeting for the express purpose of objecting to the transaction of any business because the meeting is not lawfully called or convened. Neither the business to be transacted at nor the purpose of any regular or special meeting of the board of directors need be specified in the notice or waiver of notice of such meeting.

Section 9. Quorum of Directors. A majority of the number of directors fixed by the Bylaws shall constitute a quorum for the transaction of business. The act of the majority of the directors present at a meeting at which a quorum is present shall be the act of the board of directors.

Section 10. Informal Action by Directors. Unless specifically prohibited by the Articles of Incorporation, any action required to be taken at a meeting of the board of directors may be taken without a meeting if a consent in writing, setting forth the action so taken, shall be signed by all the directors entitled to vote.

Section 11. Dissent. A director of a corporation who is present at a meeting of its board of directors at which action on any corporate matter is taken is conclusively presumed to have assented to the action taken unless his dissent is entered into the minutes of the meeting or unless he files his written dissent to such action with the person acting as the secretary of the meeting before the adjournment thereof or forwards such dissent by registered mail to the secretary of the corporation immediately after the adjournment of the meeting. Such right to dissent does not apply to a director who voted in favor of such action.

Section 12. Compensation. By the affirmative vote of a majority of directors, the board shall have authority to establish reasonable compensation for directors in payment for actual services to the corporation as directors, officers, or otherwise. A fixed sum and expenses for actual attendance at each regular or special meeting of the board may also be authorized.

ARTICLE IV
Officers

Section 1. Number. The officers of the corporation shall be a president, a vice-president, a secretary and a treasurer, as well as other additional officers whose titles and duties shall be determined by the board of directors. Any two or more offices may be held by the same person, but an officer shall not execute, acknowledge, or verify an instrument in more than one capacity if the instrument is required by law or the Articles of Incorporation to be executed, acknowledged, or verified by 2 or more officers.

Section 2. Election. An officer of the corporation shall be chosen by the board of directors. Each officer shall hold office until his death, resignation or removal as hereinafter provided. A vacancy in any office because of death, resignation or removal or other cause shall be filled by the board at either an annual or special meeting.

Section 3. Resignation and Removal. An officer may resign at any time upon written notice to the corporation. An officer may be removed at any time, either with or without cause, by the board, but such removal shall be without prejudice to the contract rights, if any, of the person so removed.

Section 4. President. The president shall be the chief executive officer of the corporation, and, subject to the direction and control of the board of directors, shall manage the business of the corporation and shall see that all orders and resolutions of the board are carried out. He or she shall preside at all meetings of the shareholders and directors and shall have such other powers and duties as may from time to time be prescribed by the board of directors or Bylaws.

Section 5. Vice-President. During the absence or disability of the president, the vice-president, or, if there are more than one, the executive vice-president, shall possess all powers and functions of the president. Any vice-president may sign, with the secretary, certificates for shares of the corporation, and shall perform such other duties as may from time to time be prescribed by the board of directors or the Bylaws.

Section 6. Secretary. The secretary shall keep or cause to be kept, at the principal executive office of the corporation, the minutes of all meetings of the shareholders and of the board of directors. The secretary shall see that all notices of meetings are given in accordance with the provisions of these Bylaws or as required by law. The secretary shall have charge of the corporate seal and shall affix it to any instrument when authorized by the board of directors. The secretary shall keep or cause to be kept, at the principal executive office of the corporation or at the office of the corporation's transfer agent, a share register, showing the names of the shareholders and their addresses, the number and classes of shares held by each, the number and date of certificates issued for shares, and the number and date of cancellation of every certificate surrendered for cancellation. The secretary shall keep or cause to be kept, at the principal executive office of the corporation, the original or a copy of the Bylaws and amendments, the resolutions of the shareholders, and other documents of the corporation, and shall certify that all such documents of the corporation are true and correct copies. The secretary shall perform whatever other duties as may be prescribed by the board.

Section 7. Treasurer. The treasurer shall have charge of the corporate funds and securities; shall keep or cause to be kept complete and accurate account books of corporate receipts and payments; deposit all money and other valuables in the name of the corporation in such banks, trust companies or other depositories as designated by the board of directors; prepare and present financial reports to the annual meeting of shareholders and the regular meetings of the board of directors, and perform such other duties as are assigned to him or her from time to time by the board of directors.

Section 8. Sureties and Bonds. If required by the board of directors, any officer of the corporation shall give to the corporation a bond for the faithful performance of his duties in such sum and with such surety or sureties as the board shall determine.

Section 9. Compensation. The salaries of the officers shall be fixed from time to time by the board of directors. No officer shall be prevented from receiving such salary due to the fact that he is also a director of the corporation.

ARTICLE V
Certificates for Shares

Section 1. Certificates. The shares of the corporation shall be represented by certificates. The form of such certificates shall be determined by the board of directors, in accordance with the requirements of the Illinois Business Corporation Act. All certificates shall be numbered and entered in the books of the corporation upon issue. They shall show the holder's name and the number of shares and shall be signed by the president or a vice-president and by the secretary and shall bear the corporate seal. In addition, they shall state that the corporation is formed under the laws of the state of Illinois and shall indicate (1) the class of shares (if there is more than one), (2) the designation of the series (if any). In the case of a lost or destroyed certificate, an affidavit of the fact shall be made by the person claiming the certificate to be lost or destroyed. The board may direct a new certificate to be issued as a replacement for that one alleged to be lost or stolen and may, at its discretion, require a bond as indemnity against any claims that may arise regarding the certificate alleged lost or stolen.

Section 2. Transfer of Shares. All certificates surrendered to the corporation by the holder of record or his authorized representative shall be cancelled and a new certificate issued to the transferee. All such transfers shall be entered in the transfer book of the corporation, kept at its principal executive office or the office of its transfer agent. No transfer shall be made within ten days preceding the annual meeting of shareholders. The holder of record of any share shall be regarded as the holder in fact for all purposes as regards the corporation.

ARTICLE VI
Waiver of Notice

Any notice required to be given under the provisions of these Bylaws, the Articles of Incorporation, or the provisions of The Business Corporation Act may be waived by the individual entitled to such notice. A waiver in writing signed by said individual, whether before or after the time stated in the notice, shall be deemed equivalent to the giving of such notice.

ARTICLE VII
Dividends

The board of directors may declare and the corporation may pay dividends on its outstanding shares from time to time, subject to the provisions of The Business Corporation Act and the corporation's Articles of Incorporation: No dividends shall be declared or paid at a time when the corporation is insolvent or its net assets are less than zero, or when the payment thereof would render the corporation insolvent or reduce its net assets below zero.

ARTICLE VIII
Amendment of Bylaws

Bylaws may be adopted, altered, amended, or repealed at any meeting of the board of directors of the corporation by a majority vote of the directors present at the meeting.

CERTIFICATE

This is to certify that the foregoing is a true and correct copy of the Bylaws of the corporation named in the title thereto and that such Bylaws were duly adopted by the board of directors of said corporation on the date set forth below.

DATED:

_____
Secretary
(seal)

APPENDIX C

Waiver of Notice
Minutes of First Meeting of Shareholders

WAIVER OF NOTICE AND CONSENT TO HOLDING OF FIRST MEETING OF SHAREHOLDERS

of

_____

We, the undersigned, being all the shareholders of _____, an Illinois corporation, hereby waive notice of the first meeting of the shareholders of the Corporation and consent to the holding of said meeting at _____ in _____, Illinois, on _____, 20 ____, at _____A.M./P.M., and consent to the transaction of any and all business by the Shareholders at the meeting, including, without limitation, the approval of the Articles of Incorporation, the recording of the Certificate of Incorporation, the approval of the preorganization subscription agreement (if applicable), and the election of directors.

DATED:

_____
Shareholder

_____
Shareholder

_____
Shareholder

_____
Shareholder

_____
Shareholder

_____
Shareholder

MINUTES OF FIRST MEETING OF SHAREHOLDERS
of

_____

The Shareholders of _____ held its first meeting on _____, 20 _____ at _____ A.M./P.M. at _____ in _____, Illinois. Written waiver of notice was signed by all the Shareholders and attached to the minutes of this meeting.

     The following Shareholders, being the owners of a majority of the outstanding shares and constituting a quorum, were present at the meeting:

_____

_____

_____

_____

_____

_____

These were represented by proxy:

_____

_____

_____

These were absent:

_____

_____

_____

     On motion and by unanimous vote, _____ was elected temporary Chairman and presided over the meeting. _____ was elected temporary Secretary of the meeting.

     The Chairman advised that the Articles of Incorporation had been filed and a Certificate of Incorporation issued by the Illinois Secretary of State. Upon the presentation of these documents to the meeting, a motion was duly made, seconded and unanimously carried that the Articles of Incorporation be approved and the Certificate recorded.

     The Chairman presented to the meeting the preorganization subscription agreement (if applicable) of the Corporation. It was read and formally approved by the Shareholders.

     By unanimous vote, the following persons were elected Directors, to hold office until the next annual meeting of Shareholders, and until the election and qualification of their successors:

NAME   ADDRESS

_____   _____

_____   _____

_____   _____

_____   _____

_____   _____

Since there was no further business to come before the meeting, on motion duly made and seconded, the meeting was adjourned.
DATED:

_____
                 Secretary

The following are appended hereto:
     WAIVER OF NOTICE OF MEETING
     COPY OF CERTIFICATE OF INCORPORATION
     PREORGANIZATION SUBSCRIPTION AGREEMENT (if applicable)
     BYLAWS

APPENDIX D

**Waiver of Notice
Minutes of First Meeting of Board of Directors**

WAIVER OF NOTICE AND CONSENT TO HOLDING OF FIRST MEETING OF BOARD OF DIRECTORS

of

_____

We, the undersigned, being all the directors of _____, an Illinois corporation, hereby waive notice of the first meeting of the board of directors of the corporation and consent to the holding of said meeting at _____ in _____, Illinois, on _____, 20 _____, at _____ A.M./P.M., and consent to the transaction of any and all business by the directors at the meeting, including, without limitation, the adoption of Bylaws, the election of officers, the adoption of the corporate seal and stock certificates, the establishment of the corporation's fiscal year, and the selection of a bank or banks where the corporation will maintain accounts.

DATED:

_____
Director

_____
Director

_____
Director

_____
Director

MINUTES OF FIRST MEETING OF BOARD OF DIRECTORS

of

_____

The first meeting of the board of directors was held at _____ in
_____, Illinois, on _____, 20_____, at _____ A.M./P.M.
The following directors, constituting a quorum of all the directors of the corporation, were present.

_____

_____

_____

_____

_____ was nominated and by unanimous vote elected temporary chairman, and presided over the meeting until relieved by the president.
_____ was nominated and elected by unanimous vote as temporary secretary, and acted as such until relieved by the permanent secretary. The secretary then presented to the meeting the Waiver of Notice of Meeting signed by all the directors, and upon a motion duly made, seconded, and carried, the waiver was appended to the minutes of the meeting.

The chairman then presented to the meeting a certified copy of the Articles of Incorporation which had been filed with the Illinois Secretary of State on _____, 20 _____. The secretary was instructed to append the copy to the minutes of the meeting.

The chairman thereupon presented to the meeting a copy of the proposed Bylaws of the corporation. . After consideration and discussion, it was unanimously

RESOLVED, that the corporation adopt as the Bylaws of this corporation the bylaws presented to this meeting.

The following persons were nominated and unanimously elected officers of the corporation to serve for one year and until their successors are elected and qualified:
_____ President
_____ Vice-President
_____ Secretary
_____ Treasurer

The president thereafter presided at the meeting and the permanent secretary replaced the temporary secretary.
Upon motion duly made, seconded, and carried, it was

RESOLVED, that the form of the corporate seal presented at the meeting, an impression of which is directed to be made by the secretary in the margin of these minutes, be and hereby is adopted as the seal of this corporation.
Upon motion duly made, seconded, and carried, it was further

RESOLVED, that the form of stock certificate submitted to this meeting be and hereby is adopted for the issuance of share certificates by the president and secretary. A copy of the stock certificate so adopted is to be attached to these minutes, and further

RESOLVED, that the principal executive office of this corporation shall be at _____
in _____, Illinois.
Upon motion duly made, seconded, and carried, it was

RESOLVED, that the fiscal year of this corporation shall end on the _____ day of the month of _____
of each year.
Upon motion duly made, seconded, and carried, it was

RESOLVED, that the treasurer be and hereby is authorized to open a bank account with
_____ located at _____ and a
resolution for that purpose on the printed form of said bank(s) was adopted and instructed to be attached to these minutes.

Upon motion duly made, seconded, and carried, it was

RESOLVED, that the Medical Reimbursement Plan presented to this meeting be and hereby is adopted as the medical reimbursement plan of the corporation.
Upon motion duly made, seconded, and carried, it was

RESOLVED, that the following annual salaries be paid to the officers of this corporation:
PRESIDENT:
VICE-PRESIDENT:
SECRETARY:
TREASURER:
   Upon motion duly made, seconded, and carried, it was

   RESOLVED, that the corporation elect to be treated as a "Small Business Corporation" for income tax purposes under Subchapter S of the Internal Revenue Code.

   RESOLVED FURTHER, that the officers of this corporation be and hereby are authorized and directed to obtain the written consent of the shareholders to the foregoing election and to file Form 2553 with the IRS.

   RESOLVED, that the officers of the corporation be authorized to sell and issue shares of stock in exchange for money and property, not to exceed $1,000,000 in amount, and further

   RESOLVED, that this sale and the organizing and managing of the corporation shall be carried out as a "Small Business Corporation," to the end that any shareholder who experiences a loss on the transfer of shares of common stock of the corporation may qualify for an "ordinary" loss deduction on his personal income tax return.
   Upon motion duly made, seconded, and carried, it was

   RESOLVED, that whereas the Articles of Incorporation authorize the issuance of _____shares of capital stock, this corporation shall sell an aggregate of not to exceed _____ shares of its capital stock at a purchase price of $_____ per share, in consideration of money paid to the corporation, as follows:
Name(s) of Purchaser(s)   Number of Shares   Amount of Money

   RESOLVED FURTHER, that this corporation sell and issue an aggregate of not to exceed _____shares of its capital stock at a purchase price of $_____ per share, upon delivery of said assets to the corporation, as follows:
Name(s) of Purchaser(s)   Number of Shares   Description of Property

   Upon motion duly made, seconded, and carried, it was

   RESOLVED, that the corporation accept the written offer dated _____, 20 _____, to transfer the assets and liabilities of said business, in accordance with the terms of said offer, a copy of which is attached to the minutes of this meeting.

   RESOLVED FURTHER, that the board of directors hereby determine that the fair market value of said business to the corporation is $_____.

   Since there was no further business to come before the meeting, on motion duly made, seconded, and carried, the meeting was adjourned.
DATED:

_____
                                   Secretary

The following are appended hereto:
WAIVER OF NOTICE OF MEETING
CERTIFIED COPY OF ARTICLES OF INCORPORATION
SAMPLE STOCK CERTIFICATE
BANK DEPOSITORY RESOLUTION FORM
MEDICAL REIMBURSEMENT PLAN (if applicable)
OFFER OF TRANSFER OF BUSINESS (if applicable)

APPENDIX E

**Name Reservation Application
Preorganization Subscription Agreement
Incorporaton Under a Close Corporation Agreement
Bill of Sale Agreement
Medical and Dental Reimbursement Plan
Articles of Incorporation for Not for Profit
Corporations**

Form **BCA-4.10** (Rev. Jan. 1999)	**APPLICATION FOR** **RESERVATION OF NAME**	**SUBMIT ONE ORIGINAL**

Jesse White
Secretary of State
Department of Business Services
Springfield, IL 62756
Telephone (217) 782-9520
http://www.sos.state.il.us

Remit payment in check or money order, payable to "Secretary of State."

Filing fee is $25 for each name reserved.

This space for use by Secretary of State

Date

Filing Fee $

Approved:

1. Name or names to be reserved (for a period of 90 days each):

_____
(Shall contain the word "corporation," "company," "incorporated" or limited," or shall contain an abbreviation of one such words)

_____

_____

2. Proposed corporate purpose:

_____

_____

_____

_____

3. Name of applicant _____

4. Address of applicant _____

     _____

5. Dated _____ , _____
                (Month & Day)   *(Year)*

     _____   _____
                                                         (Signature of Applicant)

     _____   _____

NOTE: If applicant is an individual, this application is to be signed by the applicant.

If the applicant is a corporation, this application is to be signed by the corporation's President or Vice President and verified by him and attested to by the Secretary or an Assistant Secretary.

Upon filing of this document, the name(s) will be reserved for a period of 90 days.

NOTICE OF TRANSFER
OF
RESERVED NAME

Date
Filing Fee $25.00
Approved:

The undersigned _____ hereby transfers
(Name of Original Applicant)

to _____ the right to use the
(Name of Transferee)

name _____ for corporate purposes

in Illinois. This name was reserved on _____ , _____ .
(Month & Day)   *(Year)*

The undersigned affirms, under penalties of perjury, that the facts stated herein are true.

Dated _____ , _____
(Month & Day)   *(Year)*   by _____
                                                   (Signature of Original Applicant)

attested by _____   _____
                                               (Type or Print Name)
                                 If a corporation, by its President or Vice President*

*   As the original applicant, I declare that this document has been examined by me and is, to the best of my knowledge and belief, true, correct and complete.

C-140.7

PREORGANIZATION SUBSCRIPTION AGREEMENT

We, the undersigned, severally subscribe to the number of shares set opposite our respective names of capital stock of a proposed corporation, to be known as _____ or by any other name that the members may select, and to be incorporated in the State of Illinois. We agree to pay the sum of $_____ per each share subscribed.

This subscription shall not be binding on the undersigned unless subscriptions in the aggregate amount of $_____ for shares of said corporation have been procured on or before the _____ day of _____, 20____.

All subscriptions hereto shall be payable at such time or times as the board of directors of said corporation may determine and shall be paid in cash, except as hereinafter indicated. (If any of the subscriptions are to be paid by transferring property or offering services to the corporation, a description of the property and/or services shall be attached hereto.)

Date	Name and Address	Number of Shares	Amount Subscribed

INCORPORATION UNDER THE CLOSE CORPORATION ACT

FORM
Use Form BCA-2.10 (Articles of Incorporation) and submit in duplicate. Comply with the provisions of The Business Corporation Act, discussed in Chapter 5o f this book, with the exceptions noted below.

HEADING
Add to Form BCA-2.10 a heading indicate of your election to incorporate your business pursuant to the provisions of the Close Corporation Act. For example:

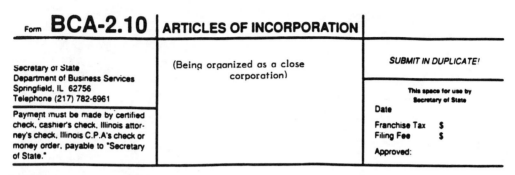

RESTRICTIONS ON TRANSFER OF SHARES
The Articles of Incorporation may list one or more restrictions on the transfer of issued shares of stock under Article Four, Paragraph 2. The stock certificates of your close corporation must either spell out the restriction(s) on the certificates themselves or state, on the face or back of the certificates, that a statement detailing the restriction(s) shall be furnished by the corporation to any shareholder upon request and without charge.

The following types of restrictions may be listed in the Articles of Incorporation.

RIGHT OF FIRST REFUSAL. This kind of restriction requires a shareholder to offer to the corporation or to one or more shareholders of the corporation or to any other designated person or to any combination of the above a prior opportunity to acquire his or her shares.
PRIOR CONSENT. This kind of restriction obligates the corporation or the holders of shares of any class of the corporation to consent to any proposed transferee of the shares.
SUBCHAPTER S TRANSFERS. This type of restriction prohibits a transfer of shares if such would cause the corporation to lose its elected status as a "small business corporation" under Subchapter S of the Internal Revenue Code.
PROHIBITED TRANSFERS. This type of restriction forbids a transfer of shares to designated persons or classes of persons, provided such a prohibition is not manifestly unreasonable.
OTHERS. Any other lawful restriction on transfer of shares may be made in the Articles of Incorporation.

MANAGEMENT OF CORPORATION BY SHAREHOLDERS
The Articles of Incorporation of a close corporation may provide that the business of the corporation shall be managed by the shareholders of the corporation rather than by a board of directors. So long as this provision continues in effect, (1) No meeting of shareholders need be called to elect directors; (2) Unless the context clearly requires otherwise, the shareholders of the corporation shall be deemed to be directors for purposes of applying provisions of the "Business Corporation Act," as now or herafter amended; (3) The Shareholders of the corporation shall be subject to all liabilities of directors.

CHANGING FROM A REGULAR TO A CLOSE CORPORATION
Any corporation organized under the Business Corporation Act of 1983 may become a close corporation by filing and recording articles of amendment of its Articles of Incorporation, which shall contain (1) a heading stating the name of the corporation and that it is reorganized as a close corporation and (2) a statement listing one or more restrictions on stock transfer from the list above. Such amendment must be approved unanimously in writing or by the vote of the holders of record of *all* the outstanding shares of each class of the corporation.

BILL OF SALE AGREEMENT

The corporation, _____, and the business owner(s) _____, hereafter called the "transferor(s)," enter into the following agreement:

    1. In return for the issuance and delivery of _____ shares of stock of _____, an Illinois corporation, I (we) hereby sell, assign, and transfer to the corporation all my (our) right, title, and interest in the following property:

    a. All the tangible assets listed on the inventory attached to this Bill of Sale, and all stock in trade, trade, goodwill, trade names, trademarks, service marks, leasehold interests, copyrights and other intangible assets (excluding--list any non-transferred assets) of _____, located at _____ Street, _____, _____ County, Illinois.

    2. In return for the transfer of the above property to it, the corporation hereby agrees to assume, pay, and discharge all debts, duties, and obligations that appear on the date of this agreement, on the books and owed on account of said business (excluding--list any unassumed liabilities). The corporation agrees to indemnify and hold the transferor(s) of said business and their property free from any liability for any such debt, duty, or obligation and from any suits, actions, or legal proceedings brought to enforce or collect any such debt, duty, or obligation.

    3. The transferor(s) hereby appoint(s) the corporation as his (her, their) representative to demand, receive, and collect for itself, all debts and obligations now owing to said business (excluding--list any unassumed debts). The transferor(s) further authorize(s) the corporation to do all things allowed by law to recover and collect such debts and obligations and to use the transferor's (s') name(s) in such manner as it considers necessary for the collection and recovery of such debts and obligations, provided, however, without cost, expense, or damage to the transferor(s).

DATED:

_____
(Transferor)

_____
(Transferor)

_____
(Transferor)

_____
(Name of Corporation)
By: _____
          (Title)

_____
          (Title)

MEDICAL AND DENTAL CARE REIMBURSEMENT PLAN
of
_____

1. BENEFITS

The Corporation shall reimburse all eligible employees for expenses incurred by themselves and their dependents, as defined in IRC S152, as amended, for medical care, as defined in IRC S213(e), as amended, subject to the conditions and limitations as hereinafter set forth. It is the intention of the Corporation that the benefits payable to eligible employees under this Plan shall be excluded from their gross income and not subject to tax, pursuant to IRC S105, as amended.

2. ELIGIBILITY

All company employees employed on a full-time basis at the date of inception of this Plan, including those who may be absent due to illness or injury on said date, are eligible employees under the Plan. A company officer or employee shall be considered employed on a full-time basis if said officer customarily works at least seven months in each year and twenty hours in each week. Any person hereafter becoming an officer or employee of the company, employed on a full-time basis, shall be eligible under this Plan.

3. LIMITATIONS

(a) The company shall reimburse any eligible employee without limitation/no more than $_____ (cross out one) in any fiscal year for medical care expenses.

(b) Reimbursement or payment provided under this Plan shall be made by the company only in the event and to the extent that such reimbursement or payment is not provided under any insurance policy(ies), whether owned by the company or the employee, or under any other health and accident or wage continuation plan. In the event that there is such an insurance policy or plan in effect, providing for reimbursement in whole or in part, then to the extent of the coverage under such policy or plan, the company shall be relieved of any and all liability hereunder.

4. SUBMISSION OF PROOF

Any eligible employee applying for reimbursement under this Plan shall submit to the company, at least quarterly, all bills for medical care, including premium notices for accident or health insurance, for verification by the company prior to payment. Failure to comply herewith may, at the discretion of the company, terminate such eligible employee's rights to said reimbursement.

5. DISCONTINUATION

This Plan shall be subject to termination at any time by vote of the board of directors of the Corporation; provided, however, that medical care expenses incurred prior to such termination shall be reimbursed or paid in accordance with the terms of this Plan.

6. DETERMINATION

The chief executive officer shall determine all questions arising from the administration and interpretation of the Plan except where reimbursement is claimed by the chief executive officer. In such case, determination shall be made by the board of directors.

NFP-102.10

(Rev. Jan. 1999)

http://www.sos.state.il.us

ARTICLES OF INCORPORATION

SUBMIT IN DUPLICATE

Payment must be made by certified check, cashier's check, Illinois attorney's check, Illinois C.P.A.'s check or money order, payable to "Secretary of State."

DO NOT SEND CASH!

(Do Not Write in This Space)

Date _____

Filing Fee $50

Approved _____

TO: JESSE WHITE, Secretary of State

Pursuant to the provisions of "The General Not For Profit Corporation Act of 1986," the undersigned incorporator(s) hereby adopt the following Articles of Incorporation.

Article 1.   The name of the corporation is:_____

Article 2:   The name and address of the initial registered agent and registered office are:

Registered Agent _____
                    First Name   Middle Name   Last Name

Registered Office _____
                    Number   Street   *(Do not use P.O. Box)*
                                                    IL
                    _____
                    City   ZIP Code   County

Article 3:   The first Board of Directors shall be _____ in number, their names and residential addresses being as follows: (Not less than three)

Director's Names	Number	Street	Address City	State

Article 4.   The purposes for which the corporation is organized are:

Is this corporation a Condominium Association as established under the Condominium Property Act?
☐ Yes   ☐ No   *(Check one)*

Is this corporation a Cooperative Housing Corporation as defined in Section 216 of the Internal Revenue Code of 1954?   ☐ Yes   ☐ No   *(Check one)*

Is this a Homeowner's Association which administers a common-interest community as defined in subsection (c) of Section 9-102 of the code of Civil Procedure?   ☐ Yes   ☐ No

Article 5.   Other provisions (please use separate page):

Article 6. **NAMES & ADDRESSES OF INCORPORATORS**

The undersigned incorporator(s) hereby declare(s), under penalties of perjury, that the statements made in the foregoing Articles of Incorporation are true.

Dated _____ , _____ .

(Month & Day)   (Year)

SIGNATURES AND NAMES   **POST OFFICE ADDRESS**

1. _____   1. _____
   Signature   Street

   _____   _____
   Name (please print)   City/Town   State   ZIP

2. _____   2. _____
   Signature   Street

   _____   _____
   Name (please print)   City/Town   State   ZIP

3. _____   3. _____
   Signature   Street

   _____   _____
   Name (please print)   City/Town   State   ZIP

4. _____   4. _____
   Signature   Street

   _____   _____
   Name (please print)   City/Town   State   ZIP

5. _____   5. _____
   Signature   Street

   _____   _____
   Name (please print)   City/Town   State   ZIP

*(Signatures must be in **BLACK INK** on original document. Carbon copied, photocopied or rubber stamped signatures may only be used on the true copy.)*

- If a corporation acts as incorporator, the name of the corporation and the state of incorporation shall be shown and the execution shall be by its President or Vice-President and verified by him, and attested by its Secretary or an Assistant Secretary.
- The registered agent cannot be the corporation itself.
- The registered agent may be an individual, resident in this State, or a domestic or foreign corporation, authorized to act as a registered agent.
- The registered office may be, but need not be, the same as its principal office.
- A corporation which is to function as a club, as defined in Section 1-3.24 of the "Liquor Control Act" of 1934, must insert in its purpose clause a statement that **it will comply with the State and local laws and ordinances relating to alcoholic liquors.**

FOR INSERTS – USE WHITE PAPER – SIZE 8 1/2 x 11

File No. _____

FORM NFP-102.10

ARTICLES OF INCORPORATION

under the

GENERAL NOT FOR PROFIT

CORPORATION ACT

of

SECRETARY OF STATE

DEPARTMENT OF BUSINESS SERVICES

CORPORATION DIVISION

SPRINGFIELD, ILLINOIS 62756

TELEPHONE (217) 782-6961

(These Articles Must Be Executed and Filed in Duplicate)

Filing Fee $50

C-157.12

Incorporation Checklist

Action	Pages where discussed	Completed
1. Select your corporate name (**Read** *Naming Your Business and Its Products and Services*; **Contact The P. Gaines Co. for trade name and trademark searches**)	53-55	
2. Prepare your Articles of Incorporation	55-62	
3. File your Articles of Incorporation	62-63	
4. Apply for corporate Employer Identification Number	74-75	
5. Notify creditors (in the case of incorporating a going business)	64	
6. Order the Corporate Record Book and Seal	65-66	
7. Prepare the Preorganization Subscription Agreement (if applicable)	66	
8. Prepare the Bylaws	66-68	
9. Prepare the Minutes of the First Meeting	68-71	
10. Issue shares of stock	71-74	
11. File Certificate of Assumed Name (if applicable)	75	

IMPORTANT ADDRESSES AND PHONE NUMBERS

ILLINOIS SECRETARY OF STATE

Corporation Division
69 W. Washington Street, Suite 1240
Chicago, Illinois 60602
Telephone (312) 793-3380

Corporation Division
The Howlett Bldg, Third Floor, Room 350
Springfield, Illinois 62756
Telephone (217) 782-6961

CORPORATE INFORMATION LINES

Name check for availability of
corporate names

Telephone (217) 782-6961 (#4) (Springfield only)

General information on filing
Articles of Incorporation, fees,
status of filing

Telephone (217) 782-6961 (#3) [Springfield]
(312) 793-3380 (Chicago)

Forms request

Telephone (217) 782-6961 (#3) [Springfield]
(312) 793-3380 (Chicago)

Annual report information

Telephone (217) 782-6961 (#5)

Photocopies and certifications

Telephone (217) 782-6875

Computer information on corporate
name, registered agent, officers,
date of incorporation, status

Telephone (217) 782-7880 (#3) Springfield
(312) 793-3380 (Chicago)

SECURITIES DEPARTMENT

Secretary of State
Securities Division
69 W. Washington Street, Suite 1220
Chicago, Illinois 60602
Telephone (312) 793-3384

Secretary of State
Securities Division, Lincoln Tower
520 South Second Street, Suite 200
Springfield, Illinois 62701
Telephone (217) 782-2256

DEPARTMENT OF REVENUE

State of Illinois
Department of Revenue
Sales Tax Division
100 W. Randolph Street
Chicago, Illinois 60601
Telephone 1-800-732-8866

State of Illinois
Department of Revenue
Sales Tax Division
191 W. Jefferson Street
Springfield, Illinois 62708
Telephone (217) 782-9488

State of Illinois
Department of Revenue
Income Tax Division
100 W. Randolph Street
Chicago, Illinois 60601
Telephone 1-800-732-8866

State of Illinois
Department of Revenue
Income Tax Division
101 W. Jefferson Street
Springfield, Illinois 62708
Telephone (217) 782-9488

Attorney General, Division of Charitable Trust and Solicitations 100 W. Randolph Street, 3rd floor Chicago, Illinois 60601 Telephone (312) 814-2595	If you plan to solicit donations, whether as a profit or not for profit, you must register with this office.

DEPARTMENT OF LABOR

Before hiring employees, apply for an Unemployment Compensation number
Department of Labor
Division of Unemployment Insurance
401 S. State Street
Chicago, Illinois 60605
Telephone (312) 793-4880
(Request New Employers' Packet)

INDUSTRIAL COMMISSION

Regarding Workers' Compensation, contact:
Industrial Commission
100 W. Randolph Street
Chicago, Illinois 60601
Telephone (312) 814-6611

DEPARTMENT OF PROFESSIONAL REGULATION

Enforcement matters, such as
Investigations and complaints:
100 W. Randolph Street, Suite 9-300
Chicago, Illinois 60601
Telephone (312) 814-4500
Website: www.dpr.state.il.us

Licensing and testing:
320 W. Washington Street, Third Floor
Springfield, Illinois 63786
Telephone (217) 782-8556

Clerk of the Supreme Court

Supreme Court Building
200 E. Capital Avenue
Springfield, Illinois 62706
Telephone (217) 782-2035

Internal Revenue Service

To pick up forms and publications in person, visit:
230 S. Dearborn Street, Lobby and 21st floor (Chicago)
7601 S. Kostner (Chicago)
Esplanade Bldg, 2001 Butterfield Road, 12th floor (Downers Grove)

To download forms from their website: www.IRS.gov
To receive forms through their fax service: (703) 368-9694
To receive taxpayer assistance: phone 1-800-829-1040

P. Gaines Co.: Website at www.PGaines.com

Zoning and Licensing

*Be sure to contact the county clerk and
the city clerk in the area in which you
live in regard to zoning and any licenses or permits
required to conduct business in their jurisdiction.*

Index

A

C

D

Treasurer
>
> See Officers

1244 stock, 70-71, 74

Tuition reimbursement plan
>
> See Tax-free benefits

U

Unemployment taxes, 22

Uniform Partnership Act, 11-12

Utility expense, deduction for business usage, 50

V

Vanguard Qualified Dividend Portfolio, 49-50

Vice-president
>
> See Officers

W

Warren, Ralph, 12

Workers' compensation insurance, 48

Write-off of $24,000, 51

COMPLETE CORPORATE OUTFIT

The P. Gaines Co. provides a complete corporate outfit with the following outstanding features:

- A corporate Records Book with padded black vinyl cover and 24K gold trim, with its matching slipcase.
- Your company name foil-stamped on the spine of the binder.
- Mylar-coated, easy-to-use index tabs, marking important divisions in the Records Book.
- 50 sheets of rag content 20-lb. bond Minute Paper.
- corporate seal stored inside its own storage box, 1 5/8" diameter. Custom finished with corporate name, state, and year.
- 20 custom printed and numbered Stock Certificates with full page numbered stubs. Each certificate is custom printed with corporate name, state, and officers' titles.

ORDER FORM—Remit with payment to The P. Gaines Co., Box 2253, Oak Park, IL 60303

For all corporate kit orders, please type or print the following information:
Corporate name exactly as on certificate of incorporaton……………………………………………
State of incorporation………………………………………………….
Year of incorporation………………………………………………
Titles of Officers who will sign share certificates (President and Secretary-Treasurer will be listed unless specified otherwise)………………………………………………………………………

Basic price of corporate outfit $71.95

8.85% Illinois sales tax (orders shipped to Illinois address only)   6.37
Choose **one** of the following two modes of shipping and cross out the other:
Shipping by UPS (delivery within 2 weeks from receipt of your order)   8.00
OR Shipping by Air Express (delivery within 3 business
days from receipt of order)   25.00
[*3-day Air Express orders must be paid for with Certified Check, Money Order, or credit card]
TOTAL_____

Ship to:
Your
name………………………………………………Address………………………………………..
                                                         (Street address required)
City…………………………………… State………………………………… Zip…………………

Charge to my: _____Visa _____Mastercard   Phone……………………………………….
Card #:_____ Expires_____
Exact name on card (please print)_____
Signature_____

For faster service, call in your credit card order at 1-800-578-3853. Total cost of the Complete Corporate Outfit via UPS shipping is $86.32, including sales tax.

Order Form

Remit check or M.O. with order to The P. Gaines Co., PO Box 2253, Oak Park, Illinois 60303

Credit Card Orders: Mail in order (supply information below) or call tollfree: 1-800-578-3853

Title	Cost	Number of copies	Total
How to Form Your Own Illinois Corporation Before the Inc. Dries! 6th, revised ed.	$31.95		
How to Form Your Own Ohio LLC* (*Limited Liability Company) Before the Ink Dries!	26.95		
How to Form Your Own California LLC* (*Limited Liability Company) Before the Ink Dries!	26.95		
How to Form Your Own Michigan LLC* (*Limited Liability Company) Before the Ink Dries!	26.95		
Small Time Operator	14.95		
Five Easy Steps to Setting Up a Retirement Plan	14.95		
Naming Your Business and Its Products & Services	19.95		
The Partnership Book	26.95		
Ohio Incorporation Manual, With Disk. 3rd ed.	31.95		
Pennsylvania Incorporation Manual. 1st ed.	24.95		
Michigan Incorporation Manual., With Disk 3rd ed.	31.95		
Indiana Incorporation Manual. With Disk. 2nd ed.	31.95		
Missouri Incorporation Manual. 1st ed.	19.95		
Minnesota Incorporation Manual. 1st ed.	24.95		
Clearing Your Business Name (Computer Search)	95.00		

> Clearing Your Business Name: **Check One**
> ☐ Company Trade Name Search   OR   ☐ Trademark or Service Mark Search
>
> Name of Product or Service _____
>
> Type of goods or services _____

Subtotal _____

8.85% sales tax (Illinois residents only) _____

Shipping ($4.40 for first book; $1.00 for each additional title) _____

GRAND TOTAL (please enclose check, M.O., or credit card information) _____

Name………………………………………………………………………………….
Address……………………………………………………………………………………...
Phone…………………………………………………
Charge to my _____ Visa _____ Master card
Card #_____ Expires_____
Exact name on credit card_____
Signature _____